UNIVERSITY OF NORTH CAROLINA
STUDIES IN THE ROMANCE LANGUAGES AND LITERATURES
Number 67

VICTOR HUGO:
A SELECT AND CRITICAL BIBLIOGRAPHY

VICTOR HUGO:
A SELECT AND CRITICAL BIBLIOGRAPHY

BY

ELLIOTT M. GRANT

CHAPEL HILL
THE UNIVERSITY OF NORTH CAROLINA PRESS

DEPÓSITO LEGAL: V. 3.238 - 1966

ARTES GRÁFICAS SOLER, S. A. - JÁVEA, 30 - VALENCIA (8) - 1967

TABLE OF CONTENTS

	Pages
LIST OF ABBREVIATIONS	11
SECTION I. Bibliographies	13
— II. Catalogues	14
— III. Editions	15
— IV. Anthologies	21
— V. Biography	22
— VI. General Criticism	34
— VII. Hugo's Political Career and Social Philosophy	48
— VIII. Language, Style, Imagery, etc.	50
— IX. Poetry	53
— X. The Novel	67
— XI. Theater	77
— XII. Foreign Influences	82
— XIII. Miscellaneous	85
ADDENDA	87
INDEX I.	89
INDEX II.	93

FOREWORD

Obviously, anyone who wishes a more complete list of publications dealing with Victor Hugo can consult such books as Thieme's bibliography, those of Dreher and Drevet, the monumental work of Talvart & Place, the bibliography of Otto Klapp, and the *MLA International Bibliography of Books and Articles on Modern Languages and Literatures*. In the following pages I have listed and commented on only those works which seemed to me desirable, important, or necessary. Not everyone will be in agreement with my choice or with my comments. I have had to exercise my judgment and hope for the best.

In order to number the entries and cross-references and prepare an index, I have had to establish a dead-line. For books, my dead-line is 1965; for periodicals, approximately September of the same year. If any item bears a later date, or if it possibly came to my attention later than it should have, it will probably be listed in the Addenda.

The place of publication is Paris, unless otherwise stated.

In the beginning, Professor R. J. Niess gave me some assistance as collaborator. He later decided to withdraw, but several items are the product of his pen, and I express my gratitude to him. I am also indebted to the Baker Library of Dartmouth College for its hospitality and its services.

ELLIOTT M. GRANT

Lyme, New Hampshire

LIST OF ABBREVIATIONS OF PERIODICALS

AUP	Annales de l'Université de Paris
CDS	Cahiers du Sud
Cr	Critique
Euro	Europe
FMod	Le Français moderne
FQ	The French Quarterly
FR	The French Review
FS	French Studies
IL	L'Information littéraire
MerF	Mercure de France
MLN	Modern Language Notes
MLR	Modern Language Review
MP	Modern Philology
NRF	La Nouvelle Revue française
PMLA	Publications of the Modern Language Association of America
RCC	Revue des cours et conférences
RDM	Revue des Deux Mondes
RFrance	La Revue de France
RGen	Revue générale belge
RHeb	La Revue hebdomadaire
RHLF	Revue d'histoire littéraire de la France
RHph	Revue d'histoire de la philosophie et d'histoire générale de la civilisation
RLC	Revue de littérature comparée
RMond	La Revue mondiale
RMus	La Revue musicale
RPar	La Revue de Paris
RR	The Romanic Review
RScH	Revue des sciences humaines
RU	Revue universitaire
Symp	Symposium
TMod	Les Temps modernes
TRO	La Table ronde

OTHER ABBREVIATIONS

B. N.	Bibliothèque Nationale
fasc.	fascicule

f⁰	folio
I. N.	Imprimerie Nationale
Mél.	Mélanges offerts à
n. a. f.	nouvelles acquisitions françaises
n. s.	nouvelle série
s.	série

I. BIBLIOGRAPHIES

1. BARRÈRE, J.-B. Vingt ans de recherche sur Victor Hugo. *IL* 13e année (4): 139-145, septembre-octobre 1961.

Strictly speaking not a bibliography but a review, with running commentary, of many studies from 1940 to 1960, accompanied by frequent suggestions of work to be done.

2. DUBOIS, P. (l'abbé) Victor Hugo: bio-bibliographie (1802-1825). Champion, 1913. 248 p.

Highly detailed, done in tabular fashion, one column dealing with events, both personal and historical; the other, bibliographical, dealing with V. H.'s publications and letters.

3. MICHAUX, F. Essais bibliographiques concernant les œuvres de Victor Hugo parues pendant l'exil. Giraud-Badin, 1930. 131 p.

Reproduces articles published in the *Bulletin du bibliophile et du bibliothécaire*, 1928-1930. M. establishes the priority of the Belgian editions for the great works of V. H.'s exile.

(Articles, too numerous to list here, dealing with V. H.'s writings before and after his exile will be found in *Bulletin du bibliophile et du bibliothécaire* from 1931 to 1939 under general title: «A travers l'œuvre de Victor Hugo. Originales, préoriginales, éditions fictives, etc.» They give information on the early printings and editions of V. H.'s writings.)

4. RUDWIN, M. Bibliographie de Victor Hugo. Les Belles Lettres, 1926. 44 p.

Limited in scope and outdated, but contains a convenient list (pp. 5-10) of articles on V. H. by 19th century writers and critics. For the latter, see also the bibliography in Maurois (No. 118). Only a few of the most important of these are included in the present bibliography; for others, see Rudwin and Maurois.

II. Catalogues

5. ———. VICTOR HUGO. Catalogue de l'exposition organisée pour commémorer le cent cinquentième anniversaire de sa naissance. Bibliothèque Nationale, 1952. 126 p.

Contains, in addition to a list of exhibited items, a study of V. H.'s manuscripts in the Bibliothèque Nationale by Mlle Suzanne Solente, and a study on V. H.'s sketches by Jean Prinet.

6. ———. Enfance et jeunesse de Victor Hugo. Ville de Paris, Maison de Victor Hugo, mai 1952. 184 p.

Prepared by J. Sergent, curator of the Musée V. H., this catalogue includes not only a list of exhibited items, but much information either on the item in question or on V. H.'s associations and activities. The brief introduction speaks fully as much of V. H.'s defects as of his virtues.

7. ———. Maturité de Victor Hugo (1828-1848). Ville de Paris, Maison de Victor Hugo, mai-juillet, 1953. 428 p.

Contains a list of exhibited items and much information either on the item in question or on V. H.'s associations and activities. A brief essay by J. Sergent deplores V. H.'s entrance into public life, but admits the value of the experience.

8. ———. Victor Hugo et les artistes romantiques. Ville de Paris, Maison de Victor Hugo, juin-septembre, 1951. 136 p., 8 reproductions.

Contains a list of exhibited items and much information either on the item in question or on V. H.'s associations and activities.

9. ———. Victor Hugo en exil. Ville de Paris, Hauteville-House (Guernesey), juin-octobre, 1955. 127 p., 8 reproductions.

Same commentary as for preceding entry, except that this catalogue gives an English translation on the opposite page.

10. ―――. Victor Hugo, homme politique. Ville de Paris, Maison de Victor Hugo, juin-octobre, 1956. 111 p.

Contains list of exhibited items ranging in date from 1821 to 1885 with a commentary on each. Many of latter give information on V. H.'s activities or associations.

III. EDITIONS

11. Œuvres complètes de Victor Hugo. Ollendorff - A. Michel, Imprimerie Nationale, 1904-1952. Gr. in-8, 45 v.

Published under the direction of Paul Meurice (1904-1905), Gustave Simon (1905-1928), and Mme Cécile Daubray (1933-1952). Each volume contains the text; as a rule, variant readings, frequently a «Reliquat», a history of the work (composition, reception, etc.), and illustrations. The edition is not completely reliable. On one occasion (*Choses vues*) the editor took the liberty of rearranging the text. The choice made by Meurice and Simon for the various «Reliquats» was sometimes arbitrary. All the variant readings are not always included. But when no genuinely critical edition is available, this edition is still an indispensable tool for scholars. There are four volumes of correspondence.

12. Œuvres complètes de Victor Hugo. Édition définitive (*Ne varietur*) d'après les manuscrits originaux. Hetzel, Quantin, 1880-1889. In-8, 48 v.

Published for the most part during V. H.'s life. No critical apparatus. Later the same publishers added 9 volumes of *Œuvres inédites*, 1886-1893, and still later 12 volumes of *Œuvres posthumes* (though most of these were reprints) 1897-1903. The combined volumes remain a satisfactory edition for general purposes.

13. Œuvres complètes de Victor Hugo. Givors, A. Martel, 1948-1955. 35 v.

Illustrated edition which contains some prefaces by Michel Braspart.

(Since 1950, when V. H.'s work fell into the public domain, many of his texts have been republished. These publications are sometimes provided with critical apparatus. It is impossible to list them all. Some — in particular those put out by the firm of Garnier and those published by Gallimard in their Bibliothèque de la Pléiade — are useful for teaching or scholarly purposes.)

14. VICTOR HUGO: Boîte aux lettres. Édition critique par Journet, R. & G. Robert. (Cahiers Victor Hugo) Flammarion, 1965. 186 p.

V. H.'s supply of insults was by no means exhausted in the published poems of *Châtiments*, as this volume proves. Its importance, however, lies in what it reveals about V. H.'s creative processes.

15. ———. Carnet. Mars-avril 1856. Texte et choix de dessins. Publié par Journet, R. & G. Robert. (*Annales littéraires de l'Université de Besançon*, v. 24) Les Belles Lettres, 1959. 59 p., 36 pl.

These notes and sketches reveal much about V. H.'s intellectual and artistic preoccupations at a time when he had major projects in view.
Review: M. Riffaterre in *RR* 51: 146-148, April 1960.

16. ———. Un carnet de Victor Hugo (1820-1821). [Présenté] par J. Gaudon in *Studies in Modern French Literature presented to P. Mansell Jones*. Manchester University Press, England, 1961. [pp. 109-132].

Text of this early notebook (B. N. n. a. f. 13441) is published in full with introduction and notes. Of some biographical and literary interest.

17. ———. Un carnet des *Misérables* octobre-décembre 1860. Notes et brouillons présentés, déchiffrés et annotés par J. B. Barrère. Minard, 1965. 281 p.

These notes and the editor's comments permit one to see V. H.'s methods of composition. They frequently illustrate how a simple phrase was developed into something more complex and effective. The book is a valuable contribution to the knowledge and understanding of V. H.'s creative genius. For a shorter treatment of the same subject, see no. 368.

18. ———. Carnets intimes 1870-1871. Publiés et présentés par H. Guillemin. Gallimard, 1953. 295 p.

Contains some inedita.
Review: G. Robert in *IL* 6e année: 74, mars-avril 1954.

19. ———. Les Châtiments 1853. Nouvelle édition publiée d'après les manuscrits et les éditions originales, avec des variantes,

une introduction, des notices et des notes, par Paul Berret. Hachette, 1932. 2 v.

Standard critical edition, indispensable for scholarly work.

20. ———. Claude Gueux. Édition critique présentée par P. Savey-Casard. Presses universitaires de France, 1956. 144 p.

Excellent edition with scientifically established and well annotated text. Illuminating introduction showing how the narrative developed from a short example to a more substantial thesis novel in which V. H. frequently departs from historical fact to make his character more appealing and his thesis more persuasive.

Reviews: Ph. Spencer in *RR* 48:291, Dec. 1957; G. Venzac in *RHLF* 58: 243-244, avril-juin 1958; H. J. Hunt in *FS* 12: 275, July 1958.

21. ———. Le Conservateur littéraire 1819-1821. Édition critique par Jules Marsan. Hachette, 1922-1938. (Société des textes français modernes) 2 v. (each in 2 parts).

Standard critical edition of this youthful review.

22. ———. Les Contemplations. Nouvelle édition publiée d'après les manuscrits et les éditions originales avec des variantes, une introduction, des notices et des notes, par Joseph Vianey. Hachette, 1922. 3 v.

Standard critical edition, but see also Journet & Robert, section IX, nos. 313-315.

23. ———. Cris dans l'ombre et chansons lointaines, edited by H. Guillemin. A. Michel, 1953. 201 p.

Inedita, much in the vein of Châtiments.

24. ———. Dieu. Édition critique par R. Journet & G. Robert. Nizet, 1960-1961. 2 v. 346 p. & 260 p.

The first volume contains the part entitled «L'Océan d'en haut»; the second reproduces the part usually called «Les Voix» but which the editors entitle «Le Seuil du gouffre.» Both include a thorough and admirable critical apparatus with an index of Hugo's language as well as the customary notes, variant readings, etc. An indispensable work for the student of V. H.'s poetry.

Reviews: M. Riffaterre in *RR* 51: 268-276, Dec. 1960; and *RR* 53: 66-69, Feb. 1962.

25. ――――. Les Feuilles d'automne. Edited by L. Bisson. Oxford, 1944. 126 p.

Good edition, though not a critical one. The text is based on that of the Imprimerie Nationale, the original manuscript having been inaccessible because of the war. Valuable notes. See also Journet & Robert, no. 316.

26. ――――. Journal 1830-1848, publié par H. Guillemin. Gallimard, 1954. 382 p.

Republishes text of *Choses vues* for period indicated, reestablishing the correct chronological order, and adding sentences and paragraphs omitted by G. Simon in the I. N. edition.
Review: E. M. Grant in *RR* 46: 302-303, Dec. 1955.

27. ――――. Journal de ce que j'apprends chaque jour (juillet 1846-février 1848). Édition critique par R. Journet & G. Robert. (Cahiers Victor Hugo) Flammarion, 1965. 280 p.

Many of these texts appeared in *Choses vues* or in *Journal 1830-1848* (no. 26), but this edition keeps them linked to V. H.'s original purpose. Edition reproduces with utmost exactitude V. H.'s diary (B. N. n. a. f. 24765, f°s 446-521). Good explanatory notes, followed by a calendar of events, personal and other, for the period in question.

Two other texts are published in Appendix (B. N. n. a. f. 24782, f°s 215-218, dated 17 fév. 1847, and B. N. n. a. f. 13423, f° 81). Former is an allegorical description of a cataract, from which V. H. concludes: «Tout a sombré, rien ne s'est perdu.» Second gives list of words dealing with light in which the vowels *a* and *e* appear.

28. ――――. Légende des siècles. Nouvelle édition publiée d'après les manuscrits et les éditions originales, avec des variantes, une introduction, des notices et des notes, par Paul Berret. Hachette, 1920-1927. 6 v.

Standard critical editon. Indispensable for scholars.

29. ――――. La Légende des siècles. La Fin de Satan. Dieu. Texte établi et annoté par J. Truchet. (Bibliothèque de la Pléiade) Gallimard, 1950; reprinted 1962. 1324 p.

Useful for the editor's comments on *La Fin de Satan;* less so for the others; in the case of *Dieu,* editor could not (in 1950) make use of critical edition by Journet & Robert (no. 24) which appeared later.

30. ———. Lettres à Juliette Drouet, 1833-1883. Le Livre de l'anniversaire. Texte établi et présenté par J. Gaudon. Pauvert, 1964. 233 p.

As indicated by Gaudon in his admirable introduction, these letters and anniversary statements constitute an extraordinary record of a sentiment which endured, in spite of some *contretemps* and even some crises, for half a century.

31. ———. Les Misérables, présentés avec les variantes des *Misères*, une introduction et des notes, par M.-F. Guyard. Garnier, 1957. 2 v. 1096 p. & 848 p.

The introduction contains careful information on genesis and composition of the novel. G.'s comments on the variant readings shed light on V. H.'s stylistic procedures. See also various studies listed in section X.
Review: H. J. Hunt in *FS* 13: 271-273, July 1959.

32. ———. Les Misérables. Édition établie et annotée par M. Allem. (Bibliothèque de la Pléiade) Gallimard, 1951. 1781 p.

Another useful edition with good notes. The latter include fragments from the «Reliquat», but the long «Préface philosophique» found at the end of the I N. edition is not given here.

33. ———. Les Misères. Edited by G. Simon. Ed. Baudinière, 1927.

The early version of *Les Misérables,* plus the 5th part not composed before 1848 which S. has nevertheless included here without manuscript marginalia and digressions. See Guyard (listed above) and Pommier (section X).

34. ———. La Muse française 1823-1824. Édition critique par J. Marsan. Cornély, 1907-1909. 2 v.

Standard critical edition of this review edited and written by V. H. and other young Romantics.

35. ———. Œuvres poétiques I. Avant l'exil. 1802-1851. Préface par G. Picon. Édition établie et annotée par P. Albouy. (Bibliothèque de la Pléiade) Gallimard, 1964. 1651 p.

Almost a critical edition with an excellent introduction, many variant readings, good explanatory notes, many inedita, and a very useful chronology. Three more volumes planned.

36. ———. Les Orientales. Édition critique avec une introduction, des notices, des variantes et des notes, par Elisabeth Barineau. (Société des textes français modernes) Didier, 1952-1954. 2 v. 170 p. & 218 p.

Standard critical edition.
Review: A. J. Steele in *MLR* 50: 543-544, Oct. 1955.

37. ———. Pierres (Vers et prose). Edited by H. Guillemin. Éditions du milieu du monde, 1951. 352 p.

Publishes a one-act comedy, *L'Intervention*. Many of the other texts are insignificant.

38. ———. Post-scriptum de ma vie, présenté par H. Guillemin. Ides et calendes, Neuchâtel, 1961. 137 p.

Includes some inedita and excludes «Contemplation suprême» which appears in the I. N. edition. G's preface is interesting.

39. ———. La Préface de *Cromwell*. Introduction, texte et notes par M. Souriau. Société française d'imprimerie et de librairie, 1897. 330 p.

Standard work, still valuable.

40. ———. Promontorium somnii. Édition critique par R. Journet & G. Robert. (*Annales de l'Université de Besançon*, v. 42). Les Belles Lettres, 1961. 200 p.

This strange, fascinating text, forming a large part of the «Reliquat de *William Shakespeare*,» is presented with skill, insight, and scholarly accuracy by the editors who include, in addition to the usual critical apparatus, a valuable index of V. H.'s language.
Review: R. Pouilliart in *Les Lettres romanes* XVIII: 369-370, Nov. 1964.

41. ———. Souvenirs personnels (février 1848-décembre 1851), réunis et présentés par H. Guillemin. Gallimard, 1952. 325 p.

Inedita, some of which are valuable, but the text is not always reliable.
Review: G. Robert in *IL*, 5e année: 104-105. Mai-juin 1953.

42. ———. Théâtre complet. Préface par Roland Purnal; notices et notes par J.-J. Thierry et Jossette Mélèze. (Bibliothèque de la Pléiade) Gallimard, 1963-1964. 2 v. 1800 p. & 1932 p.

Though not a critical edition, these volumes contain nevertheless a very useful critical apparatus.

43. ———. Théâtre de la gaîté (choix de dessins), présenté par R. Journet & G. Robert. (*Annales littéraires de l'Université de Besançon*, v. 43). Les Belles Lettres, 1961. 29 p., 30 pl.

From an album preserved at the Bibliothèque Nationale the editors reproduce 30 magnificent caricatures satirizing human types, particularly members of the army and the church. They were sketched during the last year or two of V. H.'s exile.

44. ———. Trois albums (B. N. n. a. f. 13351, 13355, 24807), choix de lavis et inventaire, présentés par R. Journet & G. Robert. (*Annales littéraires de l'Université de Besançon*, v. 55). Les Belles Lettres, 1963. 78 p., 19 pl.

Although the editors give only a choice of wash-drawings, they include a complete inventory of each album, the first of which was set up by V. H. during his lifetime, about 1854-55, the others having been constituted after his death. They point out that these *lavis* show in V. H. «le valoriste qui apparaît.»
Review: J. Seebacher in *RHLF* 65: 523-524, juillet-septembre 1965.

45. ———. Trois cahiers de vers français 1815-1818, présentés par G. Venzac. Damaze, 1952. 166 p.

Inedita which confirm the precocity of V. H.

IV. ANTHOLOGIES

46. LE CŒUR, CH. La Pensée religieuse de Victor Hugo. Bordas, 1951. 192 p.

Collection of texts by V. H. on metaphysical topics, with an interesting introduction. See also no. 505.

47. LEVAILLANT, MAURICE. L'Œuvre de Victor Hugo. Poésie, prose, théâtre. Choix, notices et notes critiques. Delagrave, 1930: revised edition 1956. 717 p.

The best one-volume anthology with excellent notes, etc.

48. MOREAU, P. & BOUDOUT, J. VICTOR HUGO: Œuvres choisies, disposées d'après l'ordre chronologique, avec une biographie, des notes critiques, grammaticales, historiques. Hatier, 1950-1951. 2 v.

Excellent selection of texts, good notes, etc. The bibliography, however, is insufficient and not always well chosen.

V. BIOGRAPHY

49. ALBALAT, A. Gustave Flaubert et Victor Hugo. *RMond* 77: 221-226, 1927.

A brief treatment of this friendship. Publishes some inedita.

50. ALLEM, M. Sainte-Beuve et *Volupté*. Malfère, 1935. 279 p.

Second chapter contains a good analysis of S-B's relations with Victor and Adèle Hugo; the third analyzes *Volupté* in the light of those relations.

51. ANGRAND, P. Victor Hugo raconté par les papiers d'État. Gallimard, 1961. 288 p.

Author utilizes unpublished documents from the Foreign Affairs Archives and from the Hugo manuscripts in the Bibliothèque Nationale as well as previous publications to relate the events of V. H.'s exile.

52. ASSELINE, A. Victor Hugo intime. Marpon & Flammarion, 1885. 316 p.

Personal reminiscences.

53. AUDIAT, P. Ainsi vécut Victor Hugo. Hachette, 1947. 353 p.

An agreable biography for the general reader.

54. BARRÈRE, J.-B. Hauteville House de Victor Hugo. *RHLF* 50: 304-315, juillet-sept. 1950.

A carefully written and interesting article. See also no. 506, and Delalande, no. 78.

55. ———. Le Voyage de Victor Hugo en Hollande, 1861. *RLC* 38: 177-202, avril-juin, 1964.

This trip was a continuation of the better-known one to Belgium (to see Waterloo). B. retraces Hugo's itinerary, reproducing much of V. H.'s *Cahier* (B. N. n. a. f. 13452).

56. ———. Hugo. L'homme et l'œuvre. Boivin, 1952; Hatier, 1962. 255 p.

Best one-volume scholarly treatment in French of V. H. and his work. Review: P. Surer in *RScH* n. s. fasc. 74: 209, avril-juin, 1954.

57. BARTHOU, L. Les Amours d'un poète. Conard, 1919; Fayard, 1924. 388 p.

Devoted primarily to V. H.'s relations with his wife and Juliette Drouet but with some mention of Léonie Biard and Blanche Lanvin. See also Escholier, no. 85.

58. ———. Le Général Hugo (1773-1828). Lettres et documents inédits. Hachette, 1926. 206 p.

Useful book on General Hugo and his son's relations with him.

59. ———. Victor Hugo élève de Biscarrat. Champion, 1925. 65 p. (Collection des Amis d'Édouard.)

Good treatment of this limited subject. Cf. Venzac, no. 137.

60. ———. Un voyage romantique en 1836. Floury, 1920. 37 p., 32 pl.

Relates V. H.'s trip to Brittany with Juliette Drouet. They were accompanied by C. Nanteuil whose sketches are reproduced. Cf. Aubrée, no. 362.

61. ———. Lettres d'Alfred de Vigny à Victor Hugo, 1820-1831. *RDM* 7e série, 25: 513-537, Feb. 1, 1925; also Émile-Paul, 1925. 77 p.

17 letters with a running commentary. For the years 1829-1831, Vigny's *Journal* contradicts the evidence of the letters.

62. BENOIT-LÉVY, E. La Jeunesse de Victor Hugo. A. Michel, 1928. 384 p.

Deals with V. H.'s parents and brothers, with V. H. himself from 1802 to 1821. Biographical and literary details. On V. H.'s political and religious opinions at this date see also Venzac, no. 137.

63. ———. Sainte-Beuve et Mme Victor Hugo. Les Presses universitaires, 1926. 595 p.

Detailed and carefully written book, but needs to be read in conjunction with Allem and Deffoux, nos. 50 & 77.

64. BERRET, PAUL. Victor Hugo.

See no. 151, section VI.

65. BIRÉ, E. Victor Hugo avant 1830. Gervais, 1883. 533 p.

66. ———. Victor Hugo après 1830. Perrin, 1891. 2 v. 296, 255 p.

67. ———. Victor Hugo après 1852. Perrin, 1894. 378 p.

These volumes are almost fanatically hostile to V. H., largely because of B's extreme conservatism in political and religious matters. They contain much information and, if used with proper caution, can still be useful.

68. BOUSSEL, P. & M. DUBOIS. De quoi vivait Victor Hugo? Éditions des Deux-Rives, 1952. 164 p.

Deals with V. H.'s finances, proving 1) that he made a fortune with his pen, 2) that, though economical, he was not, as some have maintained, miserly.

69. BRUNET, G. Victor Hugo. Rieder, 1935. 104 p.

A very short life and work for the general reader.

70. CAMBY, J. Victor Hugo en Belgique. Portraits, documents, autographes et dessins inédits. Droz, 1935. 123 p.

Good account of V. H.'s visits to Belgium.

71. CARRÉ, J.-M La Correspondance inédite de Victor Hugo et de Michelet. *RFrance* 4(4): 722-735, 1924.

Brief, excellent commentary on 11 letters. Latter now available in the I. N. edition.

72. CHARLIER, G. Une amitié romantique. Saint-Valry et Victor Hugo. Brussels, 1927.

Deals more with Saint-Valry than with Victor Hugo.

73. CHENAY, P. Victor Hugo à Guernesey. Juven, 1902. 296 p.

Personal reminiscences by Mme H's brother-in-law. Very hostile to Juliette Drouet, none too favorable to V. H.

74. CLÉMENT-JANIN, N. Victor Hugo en exil, d'après sa correspondance avec Jules Janin et d'autres documents inédits. Éd. du Monde nouveau, 1922. 196 p.

Not a detailed history of V. H.'s exile, but glimpses through his friendship with Jules Janin. Pleasingly written.

75. DAUBRAY, CÉCILE. Victor Hugo: Le Rhin. Notes de voyage. *La Nef* no. 51: 52-68, 1949.

Hitherto unpublished notes from V. H.'s *album de voyage* omitted from the I. N. edition.

76. ———. Victor Hugo et ses correspondants. A. Michel, 1947. 353 p.

Presents letters and excerpts from letters between V. H. and literary friends: Vigny, Lamartine, Dumas père, Béranger, Gautier, G. Planche. Gives an intelligent running commentary. Some inedita.

77. DEFFOUX, L. A côté du *Livre d'amour*. Les lettres de Mme Hugo à Sainte-Beuve. *MerF* 276: 265-274, Ier juin 1937.

Presents evidence that Mme Hugo became, at least for a brief period, S-B's mistress.

78. DELALANDE, J. Victor Hugo à Hauteville House. A. Michel, 1947. 182 p.

Excellent guide-book, detailed and well illustrated. Includes a catalogue of books at H. H., but for this see also Barrère, no. 54.

79. ———. Victor Hugo et la police du coup d'état. *RPar* 69: 84-94, oct. 1962.

With the aid of new documents, D. re-examines the problem of V. H.'s departure from Paris and his stay in Brussels in 1851.

80. DUCLAUX, Mme Victor Hugo. London, Constable, 1921. 268 p. French edition (Plon) 1925. 133 p.

Charmingly written biography for the general reader.

81. DUPUY, E. La Jeunesse des romantiques. Société française d'imprimerie et de librairie, 1905. 396 p.

Deals only with V. H. and Vigny. Agreeably written, scholarly, but naturally somewhat dated.

82. ÉCALLE, M. & LUMBROSO, V. Album Hugo. Iconographie réunie et commentée (Bibliothèque de la Pléiade) Gallimard, 1964. 331 p.

Good choice of pictures illustrating V. H.'s life and work, with a useful running comment.

83. ESCHOLIER, R. La Place Royale et Victor Hugo. Firmin-Didot, 1933. 194 p.

Delightful account of V. H.'s social life at no. 6 from 1832 to 1848.

84. ———. Victor Hugo raconté par ceux qui l'ont vu. Stock, Delamain & Boutelleau, 1931. 415 p.

Convenient compilation of texts from the *V. H. raconté*, Balzac's letters, Dumas' *Mémoires*, Gautier's *Victor Hugo*, Sainte-Beuve's *Mes poisons*, and others.

85. ———. Un amant de génie: Victor Hugo. Lettres d'amour et carnets inédits. Fayard, 1953. 641 p.

Complete narrative of V. H.'s relations with women from his engagement to Adèle Foucher to his old age. Nothing is left unsaid.

86. ESCHOLIER, R. Les Fiançailles d'Adèle et de Victor Hugo. *La Revue (des Deux Mondes)* 32: 650-667, 15 avril 1953.

Narrative based not only on well-known material, but also on some hitherto unpublished documents.

87. FLOTTES, P. L'Éveil de Victor Hugo 1802-1822. Gallimard, 1957. 319 p.

Based on work of Barthou, Baudoin, Guimbaud, Venzac, and others, this book combines their contributions in an interesting synthesis. Contains among other things an excellent analysis (pp. 202-240) of V. H.'s early Odes.
Review: G. Venzac in *RHLF* 59: 235-237, avril-juin, 1959.

88. FOUCHER, P. La Belle-Famille de Victor Hugo. Souvenirs de Pierre Foucher, 1772-1845. Introduction et notes de Louis Guimbaud. Plon, 1929. 246 p.

Sheds some light on character of V. H.'s parents.

89. FROMENT-GUIEYESSE, G. Victor Hugo. Éd. de l'Empire français, 1948. 2 v. 227, 244 p.

Readable, but not always accurate.

90. GAUDON, J. See nos. 16 & 30.

91. GAUTIER, THÉOPHILE. Histoire du romantisme. Charpentier, 1874. 410 p.

92. ———. Victor Hugo. Fasquelle, 1902. 292 p.

These two volumes contain anecdotes and first-hand information by V. H.'s friend and admirer. The second, published long after G's death, is drawn from previous writings. (See, *infra*, other titles by Gautier)

93. GRIFFITHS, D. A. Victor Hugo et Victor Schœlcher au ban de l'Empire d'après une correspondance inédite. *RHLF* 63: 545-580, oct.-déc. 1963.

Collection of letters with running commentary. Sheds light, not only on the relations of the two men from 1852 to 1862, but also on the divisions among the exiles, especially during the early years.

94. GRILLET, Cl. Victor Hugo spirite. Vitte, 1929; Desclée de Brouwer, 1935. 223 p.

An account of table-tipping at Jersey, followed by a critical examination of V. H.'s influence on the tables and the influence of the tables on him both as a man and as a poet. Cf. Levaillant, no. 188 and Gaudon, no. 169.

95. GUILLAUMIE-REICHER, GILBERTE. Le Voyage de Victor Hugo en 1843. France, Espagne, Pays Basque. Droz, 1936. 252 p.

Gives V. H.'s itinerary and his observations; describes his moods.

96. GUILLE, F. V. François-Victor Hugo et son œuvre. Nizet, 1950. 366 p.

Excellent book on V. H.'s son.
Review: J.-M. Carré in *RLC* 26: 401-403, juillet-septembre 1952.

97. GUILLEMIN, H. Hugo et son foyer. *TRO* nos. 20-21: 1302-1342, août-septembre 1949.

Supplementary details, based on hitherto unpublished letters between V. H. and his wife, concerning his domestic life and literary career.

98. ―――. Sur Victor Hugo et Juliette Drouet. *MerF* 307: 428-438, Ier nov. 1949.

Supplementary details, ranging from 1840 to 1878, to what was already known. One letter from V. H. evokes briefly his rôle in the June days, 1848. Two from J. D. reveal their joint anxiety and grief at the illness and death of V. H.'s grandchild.

99. ―――. «Mon père, Victor Hugo» ... d'après le *Journal* d'Adèle Hugo, à Jersey. *Le Figaro littéraire*, Feb. 19, 1955.

Some interesting inedita discovered at Hauteville House and transferred to the Musée Victor Hugo in Paris.

100. ———. Victor Hugo par lui-même. Éd. du Seuil, 1951. 190 p.

Half of this book is an essay by G. on V. H.'s personality. Other half is an anthology of texts which reveal, often indirectly, some aspect of that personality.

101. ———. Victor Hugo: lettres inédites. *TRO* no. 52: 41-61, avril, 1952.

Hitherto unpublished letters from V. H. to his family from 1861 to 1870.

102. ———. Victor Hugo et sa fille Léopoldine. *RGen* no. 55: 80-100, mai 1950.

Includes some inedita.

103. GUIMBAUD, L. En cabriolet vers l'Académie. Grasset, 1947. 184 p.

Interesting account of V. H.'s candidacies and ultimate election to the Academy, based to a considerable extent on Juliette Drouet's letters.

104. ———. Victor Hugo et Juliette Drouet d'après les lettres inédites de Juliette Drouet à V. H. et avec un choix de ces lettres. Blaizot, 1914, 1927. 504 p.

Standard treatment of this liaison. See also Souchon, no. 132.

105. ———. Victor Hugo et Mme Biard, d'après des documents inédits. Blaizot, 1927. 208 p.

Standard treatment of this intriguing subject.

106. ———. La Mère de Victor Hugo (1772-1821). Plon, 1930. 312 p.

Important for the character of Sophie Hugo and her influence on V. H. But see also Venzac, no. 224.

107. ———. Victor Hugo, l'amour et l'argent. *RPar* 56: 85-101, fév. 1949.

Relates V. H.'s difficulties between 1832 and 1838 in trying to support his two establishments.

108. HAZARD, P. Avec Victor Hugo en exil. Les Belles Lettres, 1931. 50 p. (Also *RDM* 7e série, 60: 389-420, nov. 15, 1930).

Good account of daily life during the exile.
Utilizes letters from Vacquerie to P. Maurice.

109. HUGO, ADÈLE. Journal de l'exil. *RPar* 57: 37-51, avril, 1950.

Fragments published by H. Guillemin, dealing with the period 1852-1855. See also Guillemin and Messières, nos. 99 & 119.

110. HUGO, MME V. Victor Hugo raconté par un témoin de sa vie. 1863 and many subsequent editions.

Written very probably under V. H.'s supervision, though that has been contested. Not always accurate through the frailty of human memory. Cf. G. Blaizot, «Notes sur un livre qui n'est plus négligé», *Bulletin du bibliophile et du bibliothécaire*, n. s. 15e année: 300-306, 357-367, 1936.

111. HUGO, VICTOR. Victor Hugo et ses fils. Correspondance inédite. *RHeb* 44: 261-275; 411-428; 1935.

Not all these letters have been republished in the I. N. edition.

112. JOSEPHSON, M. Victor Hugo: a Realistic Biography of the Great Romantic. Garden City, Doubleday, Doran, 1942. 514 p.

A popular biography.
Review: J.-A. Bédé in *RR* 34: 393-399, Dec. 1943.

113. LACRETELLE, P. DE. Victor Hugo et ses éditeurs. *RFrance* 3 (5, 6): 750-788; 70-97; 1923.

Treats V. H.'s relations with his publishers. Reproduces several extracts from contracts and numerous letters of V. H. Aims to destroys the legend (Biré) that V. H. ruined his publishers. Shows that V. H. was not only «correct» but even, on occasion, extremely generous.

114. LE BRETON, A. La Jeunesse de Victor Hugo. Hachette, 1928. 236 p.

A good study, still useful, even though pretty strictly limited to the biographical.
Review: M. Souriau in *RHLF* 36: 143-145, janv-mars 1929.

115. LESCLIDE, R. Propos de table de Victor Hugo. Dentu, 1885. 348 p.

Reminiscences by V. H.'s secretary.

116. LESCLIDE, J. (Mme Richard L.) Victor Hugo intime, Juven, 1902. 323 p.

Reminiscences by the wife of V. H.'s secretary.

117. MARSAN, J. La Bataille romantique. 1ere série, Hachette, 1912. 323 p. 2e série, Hachette, 1926. 286 p.

Both volumes not limited to V. H., but they help to put him in perspective, to place him in the climate of ideas and opinions, both literary and political, before (as in v. 1) and after (v. 2) 1830. Second volume also contains a section entitled «Une amitié littéraire: A. Vacquerie et V. Hugo», which not only reveals the enthusiasm of Vacquerie for V. H.'s work but gives glimpses of the immediate success of the *Légende des siècles* and *Les Misérables*.

118. MAUROIS, A. Olympio ou la vie de Victor Hugo. Hachette, 1954. 604 p. English translation by G. Hopkins, N. Y., Harper & Bros, 1956. 498 p.

A good biography, sympathetic yet reasonably objective. M. had access to some unpublished letters in addition to the vast body of printed material. Review: J.-B. Barrère in *RHLF* 56: 413-415, juillet-septembre 1956.

119. MESSIÈRES, RENÉ de. Le *Journal de l'exil* d'Adèle Hugo. N. Y., Cultural Division of the French Embassy, 1952. 38 p. (Planographed brochure).

Contains interesting and valuable quotations from manuscript owned by Morgan Library in N. Y. V. H.'s relations with other exilés, with his own family, and his intellectual differences with all of them are touched on. Cf. nos. 99 & 109.

120. MEURICE, P. Correspondance entre Victor Hugo et Paul Meurice. Fasquelle, 1909. 486 p.

Important collection of letters. Some of V. H.'s have since been published in I. N. edition, but not all.

121. PEOPLES, M. La Société des bonnes lettres (1821-1830) *Smith College Studies in Modern Languages* 5: 1-50, oct. 1923.

Relates V. H.'s relations with this conservative group.

122. PETER, R. Victor Hugo et l'Académie. *MerF* 282: 309-322, 1938.

Succinct account of V. H.'s candidacies and election. Cf. Guimbaud, no. 103.

123. SÉCHÉ, L. Le Cénacle de la *Muse française* 1823-1827. Mercure de France, 1909. 409 p.

V. H. is never in the center of the stage, but the work contains valuable details on his rôle in the founding of the *Muse française* (smaller than claimed in the *V. H. raconté*), remarks on his contributions to the *M. F.* and his epigraphs (influence of the Pléiade and Sainte-Beuve), his early relations with Lamennais, and his connections with people of classical and neo-classical tendencies.

124. SÉCHÉ, L. Le Cénacle de Joseph Delorme (1827-1830), Mercure de France, 1912. 2 v.

I. Victor Hugo et les poètes. 404 p.
Contains some details on V. H.'s family and his dazzling youth. Much attention given to his relations with Sainte-Beuve, the latters's criticism of *Cromwell*, and their final break. Treats briefly V. H.'s metrics and the Préface de *Cromwell* as a reply to Stendhal's *Racine et Shakespeare*. Good chapter on the «bataille d'*Hernani*». The book is often scattered and diffuse, but individual treatments are frequently valuable.

II. Victor Hugo et les artistes. 304 p.
Treats V. H.'s relations with David d'Angers, the Devéria brothers, Louis Boulanger (for whom V. H. had a high regard and who furnished him with material for part of *Notre-Dame de Paris*), Robelin, Delacroix, the Johannot brothers, Nanteuil, and Charlet. Does not demonstrate much reciprocal influence.

Both volumes are largely anecdotal and biographical.

125. SERGENT, J. Delacroix et Victor Hugo. *La Revue française de l'élite européenne* 17: 26-27, feb. 1964.

S. attributes the break between V. H. and Delacroix to incompatibility of temperament.

126. SIMON, G. Victor Hugo et Vigny. *RMond* 161: 227-237, 1942.

S. publishes pages on Vigny written for the *V. H. raconté* but withdrawn. Also two letters from Vigny to V. H. (This is one of a series of articles by Simon on V. H. and other literary figures in which a certain number of unpublished letters appear. The other articles will be found in the *RFrance*, 1922-1924.)

127. ———. Charles Nodier et Victor Hugo. *RMond* 177: 329-339; 178: 11-17; 1927.

Treats candidacies of both men to the Academy.

128. ———. L'Enfance de Victor Hugo. Hachette, 1904. 282 p.

129. ———. La Vie d'une femme (Mme Victor Hugo) Ollendorff, 1914. 432 p.

130. ———Chez Victor Hugo. Les tables tournantes à Jersey. Conard, 1923. 395 p.

These three books should perhaps be consulted because of the personal relations between Simon and V. H., but they have been largely superseded by Benoit-Lévy, Levaillant, Venzac, and others.

131. SOUCHON, P. Victor Hugo. Tallandier, 1949. 391 p.

Good biography which does not neglect the later years, and which treats not only the well-known works but also *Post-scriptum de ma vie*, *Dernière gerbe*, and *Océan*.

132. ———. Mille et une lettres d'amour à Victor Hugo. Gallimard, 1951. 830 p.

A large choice of Juliette Drouet's letters, with a good preface and notes.

133. ———Le Roman vécu d'une jeune fille romantique: Claire Pradier et Victor Hugo. *France Illustration. Supplément théâtral et littéraire*, 11 feb., 1950. 32 p.

Relates a touching episode in the private life of V. H. and Juliette Drouet.

134. ———. Victor Hugo journaliste. *RHeb* 44 (26): 546-560, 1935

Useful summary of V. H.'s connections with literary and political publications, and a commentary on his journalistic talent.

135. ———Olympio et Juliette. A. Michel, 1940. 253 p.

Completes Guimbaud (no. 104) on some points.

136. STAPFER, P. Victor Hugo à Guernesey. Souvenirs personnels. Société française d'imprimerie et de librairie, 1905. 250 p.

Reports some interesting conversations with V. H.

137. VENZAC, G. Les Premiers Maîtres de Victor Hugo. Bloud & Gay, 1955. 527 p.

Exhaustive treatment which discusses not only the teachers but the subjects studied. Corrects previous views on a number of points, for example, the notion that before V. H. entered the pension Cordier, his education had been unsystematic and irregular. See also in next section, no. 224.
Review: P. Moreau in *RHLF* 58: 239-242, avril-juin 1958.

VI. GENERAL CRITICISM

138. ALBOUY, P. Raison et science chez Victor Hugo. *Les Cahiers rationalistes*. no. 125, mai-juin 1952. 32 p.

A carefully composed essay reacting against recent tendency to emphasize V. H.'s mysticism.

139. ———. La Création mythologique chez Victor Hugo. J. Corti, 1963. 539 p.

Shows, on the basis of ample evidence, that V. H. possessed «une mentalité mythologique». His religious and political views were illustrated, often expressed, in mythological terms. Furthermore, while utilizing and transforming traditional mythology, V. H. tended to create his own mythology. The book is an important contribution to knowledge and understanding of V. H.'s creative genius. Cf. Py, no. 332.
Review: J.-B. Barrère in *RScH*, fasc. 117: 149-152, janv-mars, 1965; R. Journet in *RHLF* 65: 521-523, juillet-septembre, 1965.

140. AMBRIÈRE, F. Hugophobes et hugolâtres. *MerF* 260: 225-245, Ier juin 1935.

Excellent reply to two Hugophobes, Batault and Farrère.

141. AUFFRAY, A. Victor Hugo chez Don Bosco. *La Revue (des Deux Mondes)* 30: 516-525, Ier déc. 1952.

An attempt to read into V. H.'s interview with this priest a pro-Catholic tendency on the poet's part. For another interpretation see Berret, no. 154.

142. BALDENSPERGER, F. Gœthe et Hugo. Juges et parties. *MerF* 69: 25-38, Ier sept. 1907.

Interesting comparison in which B. gives the opinions each writer held about the other.

143. BARRÈRE, J.-B. Hugo. L'homme et l'œuvre. See no. 56.

144. ———. Victor Hugo et les arts plastiques. *RLC* 30: 180-208, avril-juin 1956.

Excellent article which examines, on the basis of V. H.'s prose and poetry, the relations between his knowledge and opinion of artists such as Durer, Callot, Rubens, Goya, et al., and his own sketches and poetical experience. See no. 506, and also Escholier and Sergent, nos. 167 & 215.

145. ———. Dessins de Victor Hugo dans deux carnets de la Collection Lucien Graux. *La Gazette des beaux arts*, s. 6, 58: 161-172, sept. 1961.

These two sketch-books (1856 and 1858) contain a number of satirical drawings, and many others which are either allegorical or metaphysical, verging on the hallucinatory.

146. ———. La Fantaisie de Victor Hugo. See nos. 251-253.

147. BAUDELAIRE, Ch. Victor Hugo. In his *Art romantique* (1st edition, 1868; many subsequent ones).

B. unerringly calls attention to a key trait in V. H., the attraction that the infinite had for him.

148. BAUDOIN, Ch. Psychanalyse de Victor Hugo. Geneva. Éd. du Mont Blanc, 1943. 254 p.

Freudian analysis of certain «complexes» in V. H. as revealed in his work. Interesting and provocative, but the conclusions are highly debatable.

149. BELLESSORT, A. Victor Hugo. Essai sur son œuvre. Perrin, 1929. 372 p.

Shrewd literary judgments occasionally colored by B's conservatism in political and religious matters.

150. BERRET, P. La Philosophie de Victor Hugo en 1854-1859 et deux mythes de la *Légende des siècles*. Paulin, 1910. 144 p.

B. defines V. H.'s philosophy at this period as a mixture of pythagorism, pantheism, and optimism. He examines possible sources of this doctrine, and finds an expression of it in *Le Satyre* and *Pleine mer — Plein ciel*.

151. ———. Victor Hugo. Garnier, 1927; 1939. 476 p.

Scholarly treatment of V. H.'s life and work which it separates too rigidly. Review: A. Cahen in *RHLF* 35: 455-456, 1928.

152. ———. Alexandre Weill et Victor Hugo. *Revue juive de Genève* 2: 150-155, 195-198, janv. 1934.

Discusses possible influence of Weill in introducing V. H. to the Kabbalah and in making him sympathetic to the Jews.

153. ———. Victor Hugo spirite. *RDM* 7e série, 10: 555-582, Aug. 1922.

Interesting article, but see Levaillant, no. 188, Grillet, no. 94, and Gaudon, no. 169.

154. ———. Victor Hugo et la vie future. *RDM* 8e série, 27: 345-357, May 15, 1935.

Good article on V. H.'s last two years and his belief in immortality.

155. BERSAUCOURT, ALBERT DE. Les Pamphlets contre Victor Hugo. Éd. du Mercure de France, 1912. 392 p.

B. analyzes many pamphlets and parodies, quoting some essential passages. Amusing and sometimes useful.

156. BORN, E. Victor Hugo le prophète. Éd. du Scorpion, 1962. 253 p.

What constitutes a prophet? B. examines this question and concludes that V. H. was an authentic one. In spite of this conclusion which is sound enough, the book is highly subjective.

157. BRAY, R. Chronologie du romantisme. Boivin, 1932. 239 p.

Places V. H. (and other Romantics) in the «continuité du flot littéraire emportant hommes et œuvres».
Valuable for literary history.
Review: D. Mornet in *RHLF* 43: 128, janv-mars 1936.

158. BROMBERT, V. Victor Hugo, la prison et l'espace. *R ScH*, fasc. 117: 59-79, janv.-mars 1965.

Penetrating analysis of these antithetical but complementary themes in V. H.'s work, — particularly the prison theme.

159. BUTOR, M. Victor Hugo critique. *Cr.* 21: 803-826, oct. 1965.

Illuminating article on V. H.'s intellectual curiosity, his capacity for reading, and for assimilating what he read.
Many examples given.

160. CHABOSEAU, A. Victor Hugo à Montfort-l'Amaury. *MerF* 224: 692-698, 15 déc. 1930.

Precise article on V. H.'s visits to this town, and on the composition of his «Ode aux ruines de Montfort-l'Amaury».

161. CHARLES, P.-A. Charles Nodier et Victor Hugo. *RHLF* 39: 568-586, oct.-déc. 1932.

Demonstrates that after 1827 the friendship between N. and V. H. cooled. Reproduces N's review of *Marion de Lorme,* a mixture of favorable and unfavorable criticism.

162. CORNAILLE, R. & G. HERSCHER. Victor Hugo dessinateur. Préface de G. Picon. Éditions du Minotaure, 1963. 238 p.

In spite of some errors, a useful book, for it contains a large number of reproductions, some hitherto unknown.

Review: P. Georgel in *RHLF* 65: 524-525, juillet-septembre 1965.

163. DELALANDE, J. Victor Hugo dessinateur génial et halluciné. Nouvelles éditions latines, 1964. 111 p., 121 pl.

This book complements others on this subject emphasizing rather more the hallucinatory aspect of V. H.'s drawings. Cf. nos. 167 & 215.

164. DITCHY, J. K. La Mer dans l'œuvre littéraire de Victor Hugo. Les Belles Lettres, 1925. 238 p.

The commentary is superficial; the compilation, useful.

165. DUBOIS, P. (l'abbé). Victor Hugo et ses idées religieuses de 1802-1825. Champion, 1913. 402 p.

Maintains that V. H. was never during this period genuinely Catholic. Cf. Venzac, no. 224.

166. EMERY, L. Vision et pensée chez Victor Hugo. Lyon, Audin, 1939. 136 p., 16 pl.

Traces development of the visual and visionary in V. H.'s work, and establishes a close relationship between sensations and the poet's religious thought. His metaphysics are viewed as not being carefully constructed by means of dialectal analysis and induction, but expressed through the medium of works of art. A stimulating piece of criticism.

167. ESCHOLIER, R. Victor Hugo artiste. Crès, 1926. 137 p., 111 reproductions.

E. studies the influences of various artists on V. H., then the sketches themselves. Ranking them highly, he views them as being characterized by two principal traits: «amour de la matière» and «sentiment du mystère». Some of the reproductions are in color. Cf. Barrère, Sergent, Cornaille, and Delalande, nos. 144-145, 215, 162-163.

168. EVANS, D. O. Le Socialisme romantique: Pierre Lerroux et ses contemporains. Rivière, 1948. 260 p.

Treats Leroux's social idealism, and its reflections and affinities in Romantic literature. Important for V. H. among others. See also nos. 232, 237, 242.

Review: H. J. Hunt in *FS* 3: 171-174, April 1949.

169. GAUDON, J. Ce que disent les tables parlantes. Victor Hugo à Jersey. Pauvert, 1964. 107 p.

Complements books by G. Simon, M. Levaillant, and others. Based on a recently discovered *cahier* which included a large number of table-tipping sessions from Feb. 3 to May 27, 1854. G. reproduces those not hitherto published.

170. GIESE, W. F. Victor Hugo. The Man and the Poet. N. Y. Dial Press, 1926. 315 p.

Criticism by a Hugophobe.

171. GRANT, E. M. The Career of Victor Hugo. Cambridge, Harvard University Press, 1945. 365 p.

Relates V. H.'s career and analyzes in some detail his works.
Reviews: D. Mornet in *RR* 36: 336-337, Dec. 1945; H. J. Hunt in *MLR* 41: 214-215, April 1946.

172. GREGH, F. Victor Hugo. Sa vie, son œuvre. Flammarion, 1954. 487 p.

The latest version of G.'s study of V. H., containing a new section on the poet's life, but otherwise essentially the same as his *L'Œuvre de Victor Hugo* (Flammarion, 1933, 529 p.), which is an admiring analysis of V. H.'s poetry by a poet.

173. GRILLET, Cl. See section XIII, no. 498.

174. GUIARD, AMÉDÉE. Virgile et Victor Hugo. Bloud, 1910. 195 p.

Traces the evolution of Vergil's influence on V. H.
Conscientious, useful; lacks perhaps *envergure*.

175. GUILLEMIN, H. La Bataille de Dieu. Geneva, Éd. du Milieu du monde, 1944. 246 p.

Final chapter on «Hugo et l'Église» is very good in spite of a few inaccuracies.

176. ———. L'Humour de Victor Hugo. Éd. de la Baconnière, 1951. 113 p.

Attempts, not very successfully, to demonstrate that V. H. was a humorist. But cf. Barrère, nos. 251-253 and Riffaterre, no. 459.

177. ———. Le Poète au travail (textes inédits). *CDS* 32 (no. 304): 394-412, 1950.

Contains rhymes, plans, ideas, etc. A convenient compilation.

178. ———. Présence et mystère de Hugo. *RGen* no. 17: 667-676, 1947.

Seeks to show that V. H. was «habité, dévoré par le tourment de Dieu». Underlines the conflict in V. H. between the spirit and the flesh.

179. ———. Hugo et le rêve. *MerF* 312: 5-32, Ier mai 1951.

G. recalls the dreams already published in *Choses vues,* then publishes a number from V. H.'s *Carnets.* He shows that in general V. H. had unpleasant dreams, and that though attracted to the world of dreams, he did not exploit this realm as he might have.

180. GUYAU, J. M. L'Art au point de vue sociologique. Alcan, 1914. 387 p.

Contains a good chapter (IV, 190-249) on the philosophical and social import of V. H.'s work.

181. HEUGEL, J. Essai sur la philosophie de Victor Hugo, suivi de réflexions sur le même thème. Calmann-Lévy, 1952. 355 p.

Reproduces with some changes and additions an earlier study (1932). A supplementary section treats topics like «H. et le progrès», «H. et le spiritisme». Rather superficial. To be read in connection with Renouvier, Levaillant, and Hunt, nos. 200, 188, 237.

182. HOFMANNSTHAL, H. von. Essai sur Victor Hugo. Droz, 1937. 87 p. (Traduit de l'allemand par M. Ley-Deutsch.)

Interesting interpretation of V. H.'s mind and work, emphasizing the «sens du grand» which always inspired him.

183. HOOKER, K. W. The Victor Hugo Legend. *RR* 27: 190-200, July-dec. 1936.

Hostile article apparently largely inspired by Biré.

184. LECONTE DE LISLE, Ch. Victor Hugo in *Les Poètes contemporains.* Originally published in *Le Nain jaune,* 1864; repub-

lished in 4th volume of his *Œuvres* (pp. 257-263), A. Lemerre, 1899.

Very perceptive criticism of V. H.'s poetry.

185. ———. Discours sur Victor Hugo in v. 4 (pp. 287-309) of his *Œuvres*, A. Lemerre, 1899.

This is the «Discours de réception» delivered at the French Academy (31 mars 1887) when Leconte de Lisle was chosen to occupy V. H.'s chair. Somewhat more superficial than the preceding study.

186. LEGAY, T. Victor Hugo jugé par son siècle. Éd. de la Plume, 1902. 640 p.

A still useful compilation. See also Escholier, no. 84.

187. LEVAILLANT, M. Victor Hugo, Juliette Drouet et «Tristesse d'Olympio» d'après des documents inédits. Delagrave, 1945. 126 p.

Reprint of an earlier study (1928) which revealed how closely this poem is connected with V. H.'s personal life. Some additions, in particular, ch. 8, «L'Apothéose du souvenir». Important work for interpretation of this poem.

188. ——— La Crise mystique de Victor Hugo 1843-1856. Corti, 1954. 296 p.

Supersedes articles by same author in *RLC* and *La Revue (des Deux Mondes)*. Important, not only for V. H.'s belief in spiritualism, but also for *Les Contemplations*, especially book VI. Cf. Grillet, no. 94.
Reviews: H. J. Hunt in *FS* 10:270-271, July 1956; J.-B. Barrère in *RScH* n. s., fasc. 80: 533-535, oct-déc. 1955.

189. MALLION, J. Victor Hugo et l'art architectural. Les Presses universitaires de France, 1962. 743 p.

Through V. H.'s published work and through the minutes of the Comité des Arts et Monuments of which V. H. was a member, M. not only traces the poet's archeological and architectural knowledge and views, but evaluates them.
Review: R. Baschet in *RHLF* 64: 687-689, oct.-déc. 1964.

190. MARÉCHAL, C. Lamennais et Victor Hugo. Savaète, 1905. 152 p.

To be used with caution, as it exaggerates the influence of Lamennais on V. H.

191. MARMIER, J. Victor Hugo et Horace avant 1840. *Les Lettres romanes* XVIII: 3-27, fév. 1964.

192. ―――. Victor Hugo et Horace après 1840. *Les Lettres romanes* XVIII: 137-163, mai 1964.

These two articles contain a good survey of the problem, showing that the most interesting period in which V. H. was influenced by Horace was that of 1840-1870. M. suggests that finally — in V. H.'s old age — Horace supplanted Vergil in the poet's esteem. The first article gives in appendix three hitherto unpublished verse translations made by V. H. in 1817-1818.

193. MARSAN, J. La Bataille romantique. See no. 117.

194. MOORE, O. H. Victor Hugo as a Humorist before 1840. *PMLA* 65: 133-153, March 1950.

A repertory of V. H.'s use of laughter and his attempts at humor. Neither Moore nor Guillemin (no. 176) has wholly succeeded in proving that V. H. possessed much of a comic gift. But cf. Barrère, nos. 251-253 and Riffaterre, no. 459.

195. MOREAU, P. Le Classicisme des romantiques. Plon, 1932. 409 p.

V. H. appears frequently, but no single section is devoted exclusively to him. Ch. 4, pt. III gives brief treatment to V. H.'s classical education, the classical orientation of contributors to *La Muse française*, classical and neo-classical vocabulary and mannerism of V. H.'s *Odes* and his other early writings, and demonstrates that he often called on the classics to justify his theories. Ch. 6 treats his use of classical devices (and justifications) in his plays.

196. PÉGUY, Ch. Sur Victor Hugo (Fragment de 1914). *CDS* 31 (no. 300): 209-214, 1950.

Views V. H. as a classicist by nature forcing himself to be a romantic. Debatable.

197. POULET, G. L'Espace et le temps chez Victor Hugo. *Esprit* 18 (2): 478-505, 1950.

Interprets V. H.'s universe as «tourbillonnant» and essentially chaotic. Interesting, but highly debatable. Cf. Hoog, no. 308.

198. ———. La Distance intérieure. Plon, 1952. 355 p.

Contains a section on V. H. See preceding entry.

199. RAYMOND, M. Hugo mage in his *Génies de France*, Neuchâtel, Éd. de la Baconnière, 1942. 248 p.

Brilliant chapter on V. H. as a seer and as a metaphysical poet.

200. RENOUVIER, Ch. Victor Hugo le philosophe. Colin, 1900. 378 p.

Stimulating and still useful discussion of V. H.'s ideas. R. takes V. H. seriously as a thinker.

201. RIFFATERRE, M. La Vision hallucinatoire chez Victor Hugo. *MLN* 78: 225-241, may 1963.

Penetrating analysis of the question in which R. shows how V. H.'s vision and technique dissolve «la surface figée des apparences pour pénétrer plus avant que ne font la raison et les sens, jusqu'au surréel».

202. ———. Victor Hugo, Critic of Shakespeare. *The American Society Legion of Honor Magazine* 31 (3): 139-152, 1960.

Brief but penetrating glimpse into V. H.'s book on Shakespeare. R. states that V. H.'s «own genius gave him special insights into the nature of poetry», — hence, into that of Shakespeare.

203. ———. Victor Hugo and the Universe within the Poet. *The American Society Legion of Honor Magazine* 35 (1): 11-27, 1964.

Valuable article which demonstrates that the skull image and theme in V. H.'s work are «but the stylistic form of a philosophical attitude».

204. ROLLAND, Romain, AND OTHERS Victor Hugo. Special number of *Europe* 38: 153-331, June 15, 1935.

Articles by Romain Rolland, H. Mann, Alain, Cassou, Guéhenno, Lalou, Raymond, Saurat, Soupault, Bloch, and others. Interesting judgments, essentially favorable, on V. H.

205. Roos, J. Les Idées philosophiques de Victor Hugo. Ballanche et Victor Hugo. Nizet, 1958. 155 p.

Author discerns a definite parallelism of ideas and doctrines in Ballanche and V. H. Both were concerned with human suffering, the existence of evil, and the nature of God. Both were what he calls «rational mystics». The book was composed, according to the Avant-propos, in 1946, but author did not take into consideration studies which appeared between then and date of publication.

206. Rousselot, J. Victor Hugo, notre contemporain (pp. 35-45) in *Présences contemporaines*. Nouvelles éditions Debresse, 1958.

R. detects in V. H. the attempt, forecasting that which certain 20th century writers are making, to reconcile «intelligence with sensibility, ephemeral man with eternal nature, arbitrary creation with the patience of God.»

207. Rudwin, M. Satan et le satanisme dans l'œuvre de Victor Hugo. Les Belles Lettres, 1926. 150 p.

Not always accurate, and treats too briefly an important question. Cf. Zumthor, no. 356.
Review: F. Baldensperger in *RLC* 7: 193-196, janv.-mars, 1927.

208. Saint-Denis, E. de Victor Hugo et la mer anglo-normande. *Les Études classiques* 31: 275-294, juillet 1963.

A good survey, from which author concludes that V. H.'s sea-poetry is that of a visionary but at the same time is based on direct observation; furthermore, that the sea which appears in the works written during the Jersey-Guernsey period is a special sea: «la mer anglo-normande, capricieuse et antithétique, épique et apocalyptique.»

209. Saulnier, V. L. Victor Hugo et la Renaissance. *AUP* 24: 191-211, avril-juin 1954.

Convenient survey of this question, showing that V. H. found in the Renaissance an admirable *décor*, impressive personalities, and on at least one occasion an important myth («Le Satyre»).

210. SAURAT, D. L'Expérience de l'au-delà. La Colombe, Ed. du Vieux Colombier, 1951. 192 p.

Part of this book examines sympathetically V. H.'s table-tipping experiences at Jersey. Cf. Grillet and Levaillant, nos. 94 & 188.

211. ―――. La Religion de Victor Hugo. Hachette, 1929. 212 p.

Presents a highly debatable interpretation of V. H.'s attitude on religion; sees in V. H.' a «grand primitif fondateur de religion.» Cf. Uitti, no. 349.
Reviews: A. Schinz in *RHLF* 39: 569-602, oct.-déc. 1932; J. Wahl in *NRF* 35: 559-562, oct. 1930.

212. SAURAT, D. Victor Hugo et les dieux du peuple. La Colombe, 1948. 347 p.

First part of this book is reprint of preceding entry: second part, «Les Dieux du peuple,» compares V. H. with Spenser, Milton, Blake. Interesting; also debatable.

213. SCHENCK, E. M. La Part de Charles Nodier dans la formation des idées romantiques de Victor Hugo jusqu'à la Préface de *Cromwell*. Champion, 1914. 150 p.

Useful study, though it tends to exaggerate N's rôle.
Review: E. Estève in *RHLF* 23: 624-625, oct.déc. 1916.

214. SCHWAB, R. La Renaissance orientale. Payot, 1950. 526 p.

A previous study: «Hugo troublé par l'Inde» (*RLC* 21: 497-511, 1947) is reprinted here with some minor changes and additions. Work is important for oriental influence on V. H. (among others).
Reviews: J.-M. Carré in *RLC* 25: 149-152, janv.-mars 1951; J. Seznec in *RHLF* 53: 236-237, avril-juin 1953.

215. SERGENT, J. Dessins de Victor Hugo. Éd. de la Palatine, Plon, 1955. 69 p., 23 reproductions.

Like Escholier (no. 167), S. argues that V. H.'s sketches are the work of a first-rate artist. He underlines their dramatic and intellectual qualities as well as their rendition of the visual and the visionary. Cf. nos. 144-145.
Review: J.-A. Bédé in *FR* 32: 94-95, oct. 1958.

216. STAPFER, P. Racine et Victor Hugo. Colin, 1887. 324 p.

Still highly readable essay with some criticism that has stood the test of time.

217. TEMPLE-PATTERSON, H. Petites clefs de grands mystères (Victor Hugo, Jean-Paul Richter et Sébastien Mercier). *RLC* 25: 85-100, janv-mars 1951.

Good article on the source of certain Hugolian symbols and themes (such as the rain of blood, battlefields, etc.).

218. ———. Poetic Genesis: Sébastien Mercier into Victor Hugo. Vol. XI in *Studies on Voltaire and the 18th Century*. Institut et Musée Voltaire, Les Délices, Geneva, 1960. 315 p.

Demonstrates that in many respects Mercier was a precursor of V. H. and influenced him to some extent.
Review: E. M. Grant in *MLN* 76: 279-281, March, 1961.

219. THIBAUDET, A. Situation de Victor Hugo. *RPar* 42(3): 258-284, May 15, 1935.

Excellent critical statement of V. H.'s contribution to French letters. T. gives high rank to Hugo's genius and justifies this by a brief but penetrating look at V. H.'s principal works.

220. ———. Victor Hugo était-il intelligent? *NRF* 43: 590-597, Sept. 1, 1934.

Refutes effectively those who claim that V. H. was not intelligent.

221. THIÉBAUT, M. Victor Hugo 1954. *RPar* 61(1): 140-152, juin 1954.

Taking A. Maurois' *Olympio* as point of departure, T. states well the attitude of many educated Frenchmen of the 1950's toward V. H.

222. TINT, H. The Status of Hugo, according to Neo-Kantian Aesthetics: a Study of Renouvier as Literary Critic. *MLR* 53: 344-354, July 1958.

T. analyzes R's neo-Kantian aesthetics in which morality plays an essential role and concludes that on this basis «Hugo's stature as an artist is impressive.»

223. TORTEL, J. Notions sur l'esthétique de Victor Hugo. *CDS* 35 (no. 311): 19-36, 1952.

By well-chosen quotations from V. H.'s work, T. suggests some of the central notions of the poet's aesthetics.

224. VENZAC, G. Les Origines religieuses de Victor Hugo. Bloud & Gay, 1955. 679 p.

Latest and best treatment of this question, shedding new light on V. H.'s religious and political opinions before 1825 as well as on the source of those opinions, See also Dubois, no. 165.
Review: P. Moreau in *RHLF* 58: 239-242, avril-juin 1958.

225. ———. Les Premiers Maîtres de Victor Hugo. See no. 137.

226. VIATTE, A. Victor Hugo et les illuminés de son temps. Montreal, Ed. de l'Arbre, 1942. 284 p.

Traces in V. H.'s work the influence of illuminati like Fabre d'Olivet, Fourier, and others. Well documented, interesting, but the conclusions are debatable.
Review: S. David in *FR* 16: 439-441, March 1943.

227. ———. Le Catholicisme chez les Romantiques. Boccard, 1922. 401 p.

Contains an interesting chapter on Nodier and V. H. Cf. Venzac, no. 224.

228. VINCHON, J. La Tache et les dessins de Victor Hugo. *La Gazette des beaux arts*, s. 6, 58: 153-160, Sept. 1961.

Vinchon, a psychiatrist, argues that Hugo was not a genuine Tachist, that in very few of his drawings are blobs (taches) accidental; rather, they are a part of his skilled technique.

229. WEBER, J.-P. Genèse de l'œuvre poétique. (Bibliothèque des idées) Gallimard, 1960. 563 p.

One chapter (pp. 91-184) devoted to V. H. It attempts to show that a «souvenir unique'» that of a picture representing the *Mäusethurm* (*la Tour des rats*) which hung over V. H.'s bed in his childhood, is the origin of certain themes in his work: the themes of a fiery sky, of a dilapidated tower, of the monstrous birth of living creatures, and of the *portail-visage* or *visage-dans-la-cathédrale*.

VII. Hugo's Political Career and Social Philosophy

230. Ascoli, G. L'Évolution politique de V. Hugo jusqu'à l'exil. *AUP* 11: 138-161, mars-avril 1936.

    Fair-minded treatment, but much too brief on the Second Republic.

231. Benoit-Guyod, G. V. Hugo pair de France. *RDM* 8e s., 39: 773-811, 15 juin 1937.

    Fairly detailed account of V. H.'s appointment as Peer and his càreer in that capacity. Seeks to show that he was more liberal in his views than most of his confreres.

232. Evans, D. O. Social Romanticism in France 1830-1848. Oxford, 1951. 149 p.

    Shows the reflection of liberal and socialistic thought in V. H. (among others). Cf. Picard, no. 242.

233. Grant, E. M. Exile's Return. *RR* 30: 382-410, Dec. 1939.

    Treats in some detail V. H.'s attitude and activity during the war of 1870 and the Commune.

234. Grant, E. M. Victor Hugo during the Second Republic. *Smith College Studies in Modern Languages* 17: 1-68, Oct. 1935.

    Detailed account of V. H.'s political views and activity during this period. Combats interpretation of Lacretelle, no. 240.

235. Guyau, J. M. See no. 180.

236. Hamelin, J. See no. 499.

237. Hunt, H. J. L'Impulsion socialiste dans la pensée politique de Victor Hugo. *RHLF* 25: 209-223, avril-juin, 1933.

    Effective reply to Schinz (no. 250), showing that V. H. was long motivated by humanitarian ideals, and after 1851 became a sincere republican.

238. ———. Le Socialisme et le romantisme en France. Étude de la presse socialiste de 1830 à 1848. Oxford, 1935. 399 p.

Important work on this general question with one section devoted to «Les grands poètes socialisants» including V. H.
Review: M. E. I. Robertson in *MLR* 32: 113-114, Jan. 1937.

239. Isay, R. Victor Hugo européen. *La Revue (des Deux Mondes)* 31: 87-108, 1er janv 1953.

Calls attention to V. H.'s European formation as well as to his conception of the United States of Europe.

240. Lacretelle, P. de Vie politique de Victor Hugo. Hachette, 1928. 254 p.

Hostile and prejudiced, but contains much information. Cf. Hunt and Grant, nos. 237 & 234.

241. Moreau, P. Horizons internationaux de Victor Hugo. *RLC* 26: 289-295, juillet-septembre 1952.

Brief but suggestive on the breadth of V. H.'s outlook.

242. Picard, R. Le Romantisme social. N. Y., Brentano, 1944. 437 p.

Contains a good chapter on «V. H. homme politique et poète social.»

243. Pommier, J. Les Écrivains devant la révolution de 1848. Les Presses universitaires, 1948. 77 p.

Contains a convenient summary (pp. 58-68) of V. H.'s activities from February to December 1848.

244. Rozelaar, L. Le Mémorial de Sainte-Hélène et Victor Hugo en 1827. *FQ* 9: 53-68, 1927.

245. ———. Le Mémorial de Sainte-Hélène et Victor Hugo après 1827. *FQ* 10: 130-155, 1928.

In these two articles author clearly establishes the influence of this book on V. H. before 1848.

246. RUSHWORTH, F. D. Victor Hugo and his Marxist Critics. *FS* 4: 333-344, Oct. 1950.

Traces attitude of marxists toward V. H. from Marx himself to Aragon.

247. SAVEY-CASARD, P. Le Crime et la peine dans l'œuvre de Victor Hugo. Les Presses universitaires, 1956. 424 p.

Traces the evolution of V. H.'s ideas on crime and punishment, characterizes the various types of criminals in his work, showing throughout the influence of his political career on his social thought. Concludes that while V. H. did not contribute directly to penal science, he stirred the conscience of men. Thorough and scholarly. Bibliography: 395-413. No index.
Reviews: G. Venzac in *RHLF* 58: 242-243, avril-juin 1958; J.-B. Barrère in *RLC* 31: 583-585, oct.-déc. 1957.

248. ―――. L'Évolution démocratique de Victor Hugo. *RHLF* 60: 316-333, juillet-septembre, 1960.

In general, good analysis of the problem, though weak on the political details of 1848-1851 in so far as they concern V. H. Author concludes correctly that Hugo's «démocratie a pour âme la fraternité.»

249. ―――. Le Pacifisme de Victor Hugo. *RLC* 35: 421-432, juillet-septembre 1961.

Accurate analysis of the evolution of V. H.'s ideas on war and peace.

250. SCHINZ, A. L'Unité dans la carrière politique de Victor Hugo. *RHLF* 39: 15-44, janv-mars 1932.

Utilizes Lacretelle (no. 240) to claim that V. H. was consistently antidemocratic throughout his career. For opposite view, see Hunt, Grant, and Savey-Casard, nos. 237, 234, 248.

VIII. LANGUAGE, STYLE, IMAGERY, ETC.

251. BARRÈRE, J.-B. La Fantaisie de Victor Hugo 1802-1851. Corti, 1949. v. 1. 447 p.

252. ―――. La Fantaisie de Victor Hugo 1852-1885. Corti, 1960. v. 2. 508 p.

253. ———. La Fantaisie de Victor Hugo. Thèmes et motifs. Corti, 1950. v. 3. 288 p.

These three volumes constitute an important contribution to Hugo scholarship. They establish and analyze admirably a vein in V. H.'s work that previous critics have not always recognized. Indispensable for a proper and thorough understanding of V. H.'s work.
Reviews: H. J. Hunt in *FS* 4: 81-82, Jan. 1950; *FS* 6: 81-83, Jan. 1952; *FS* 16: 74-77, Jan. 1962.

254. BRUNEAU, CH. L'Époque romantique. Vol. XII of the *Histoire de la langue française des origines à nos jours* by F. Brunot. A. Colin, 1948. 593 p.

One section deals with the «Préface de *Cromwell*,» treating its importance as one item in the history of the French language. Other sections analyze the vocabulary and style of the Romantic writers including, of course, V. H. Contains a valuable bibliography (pp. ix-xix).
Review: A. Ewert in *FS* 3: 267-268, July, 1949.

255. BRUNOT, F. Les Romantiques et la langue poétique. *RPar* 35(6): 309-331, nov-déc, 1928.

To show how the poetic language was renewed by the Romantic writers, B. draws most of his examples from V. H.

256. DUVAL, G. Dictionnaire des métaphores de Victor Hugo. Piaget, 1888. 326 p.

Very limited in scope, hence only moderately useful.

257. GRÉGOIRE, E. L'Astronomie dans l'œuvre de Victor Hugo. Droz, 1933. 249 p.

A study of metaphors and similes suggested by sky, stars, etc. Useful within this limit.
Review: P. Berret in *RHLF* 41: avril-juin, 1934.

258. HUGUET, ED. Les Métaphores et les comparaisons dans l'œuvre de Victor Hugo. Hachette, 1904-1905. 2 v. 390, 397 p.

First volume classifies V. H.'s figures of speech involving form or shape (geometrical figures, animals, parts of body, deformities, etc.), gives numerous examples with a commentary. Second volume classifies those involving color,

light, or shade (sky, stars, dawn, sunset, night, snow, ice, etc.), and again gives exemples with commentary. More a dictionary of figures of speech than a study.
Reviews: F. Baldensperger in *Revue critique d'histoire et de littérature* 59: 153-155, 1905; 61: 15, 1906.

259. JOUSSAIN, A. L'Esthétique de Victor Hugo. Le pittoresque dans le lyrisme et dans l'épopée. Société française d'imprimerie et de librairie, 1915; Boivin, 1920. 223 p.

J. defines the picturesque as the evocation of a given aspect of the external world presented to our imagination by the writer in the form of a picture. Examining V. H.'s work in the light of this definition, he concludes that V. H.'s sensibility led him in the period before 1850 to a «poésie imagée et colorée» more than to a «poésie pittoresque.» Later, under the influence of his philosophy, the picturesque is affected by the visionary.

260. LE DÛ, A. Les Rythmes dans l'alexandrin de Victor Hugo. La répétition symétrique, de 1815 à 1856. Hachette, 1929. 205 p.

261. ———. Le Rythme dans la prose de Victor Hugo. Le groupement ternaire, de 1818 à 1831. Hachette, 1929. 408 p.

Both volumes contain good analyses which show V. H.'s tendency to use «la triple série dans l'idéation, dans la composition, dans l'expression.»
Review: P. Berret in *RHLF* 38: 124-125, avril-juin, 1931.

262. MARTIN, E.-L. Les Symétries de la prose dans les principaux romans de Victor Hugo. Les Presses universitaires, 1925. 131 p.

Interesting study showing that V. H. possessed art of varying length and compositon of his sentences, at the same time arranging «d'agréables symétries.» Among the latter, the «symétries de soulignement» (repetitions, parallelisms, contrasts, etc.) tended to increase from 1819 to 1862, as, interestingly, did the number of short sentences.

263. MEYER, E. Un cas d'incontinence verbale: *L'Homme qui rit* de Victor Hugo. *RCC* 2e série, 27: 743-757, 1926.

Stylistic study of two passages by a critic who obviously does not admire V. H.

264. ROBERTSON, M. E. I. L'Épithète dans les œuvres lyriques de Victor Hugo publiées avant l'exil. Jouve, 1926; Champion, 1927. 559 p.

Interesting and valuable study which not only treats the question of style, but through it touches on aesthetics. Author shows that V. H. outstripped his predecessors in developing epithets other than adjectival ones, and that his epithets tell us a good deal about his personality, his sensibility, his critical faculties. Numerous examples given in support.
Review: L. Refort in *RHLF* 35: 452-454, juillet-septembre 1928.

265. ROCHETTE, A. L'Alexandrin chez Victor Hugo. Hachette, 1911. 605 p.

Seeks to prove by long analysis that V. H.'s poetry is far less revolutionary in its rhythms than in style, vocabulary, imagery, and thought.

266. TEMPLE-PATTERSON, H. The Origin of Hugo's Condensed Metaphors. *FS* 5: 343-348, Oct. 1951.

Author sees quite plausibly the origin of V. H.'s two noun metaphors in L.-S. Mercier. See also no. 218.

267. ULLMANN, E. DE. La Transposition dans la poésie lyrique de Hugo des *Odes et ballades* aux *Contemplations*. *FMod* 19: 277-295, oct 1951.

U. shows that well before Baudelaire, V. H. practised the technique of «correspondances.» Analyzes V. H.'s use of this technique (For possible influence of V. H. on Baudelaire's theory, see J. Pommier, *La Mystique de Baudelaire*, 1932, pp. 16-23).

268. ULLMANN, S. Style in the French Novel. Cambridge University Pres, 1957. 273 p.

Deals only briefly with V. H., but comments on V. H.'s use of local color in *Notre-Dame de Paris* are useful.

IX. POETRY

269. ALBOUY, P. Une œuvre de V. Hugo reconstituée. *RHLF* 60: 388-423, juillet-septembre 1960.

Author has put together a poem written by V. H. about 1857-1858 but never published as a complete unit. It was cut up and sections utilized in

Toute la lyre, Les Quatre Vents de l'esprit, and other volumes. Complete original would have been a meditation on '93 and the rôle of violence in history.

270. ———. Aux commencements de *La Légende des siècles. RHLF* 62: 565-572, oct.-déc. 1962.

Commentary on a fragment of manuscript found in the «Reliquat» of the *Légende des siècles.* Throws some light on V. H.'s earliest intentions.

271. Ascoli, G. A propos du «Rouet d'Omphale» de V. Hugo. *Mél. Ed. Huguet* (pp. 351-362) Boivin, 1940.

Argues plausibly that Mme Biard was the inspiration for this poem.

272. Barineau, E. *Les Feuilles d'automne* et les *Mémoires de Lord Byron. MP* 55: 217-238, May 1958.

Proves that certain epigraphs in the *F. d'a* come from these *Mémoires* and that the subject of «Dédain» was inspired by them; argues convincingly that certain themes such as the loss of youth, the loss of friends through death or absence, etc. were enriched by these *Mémoires.* First two vols. published in 1830 naturally more influential on V. H. than those published in 1831.

273. ———. *Les Feuilles d'automne*: l'intime et l'universel. *MP* 58: 20-40, August 1960.

B. shows that in many poems of this *recueil* V. H. attributes universal significance to his own personal feelings and experiences. Her opinion that the effect is often «déplaisant» is perhaps debatable.

274. Barrère, J.-B. La Fantaisie de Victor Hugo. See nos. 251-253.

275. ———. Promenade dans un album de voyage de Victor Hugo (1865). *RHph* (now *RScH*) fasc. 41: 1-48, janv-mars 1946; fasc. 43: 244-284, juillet-septembre, 1946.

B. establishes V. H.'s itinerary for his 1865 trip to Belgium and the Rhineland; reproduces many of the verses jotted down in the album. Important for the *Chansons des rues et des bois.* Cf. no. 506.

276. ———. Victor Hugo dans l'île de Serk. Mai-juin 1859. *RScH* n. s. fasc. 74: 117-165, avril-juin 1954.

Utilizing V. H.'s *album de poche*, B. relates admirably the poet's visit to Sark in 1859 and shows the rôle that visit played in the composition of the *Chansons des rues et des bois, Les Travailleurs de la mer,* and *Le Théâtre en liberté.* Cf. 506.

277. ———. Hugo et le chèvre-pied. *Cahiers de l'Association internationale des études françaises,* no. 10: 121-137, mai 1958.

Rapid review of the theme of satyrs and fauns in V. H.'s work leading to the conclusion that the poet's sensibility was in part pagan.

278. ———. Hypothèse sur la psychologie des *Contemplations. Annals of the Faculty of Arts,* Ibrahim Pasha University, 1, 1951.

Emphasizes the conflict in V. H. between sensuality and spiritualism as a key to the understanding the *Contemplations.*

279. BAUDOIN, CH. Deux épopées de la rédemption. L'influence de la *Divine épopée* d'Alexandre Soumet sur la *Fin de Satan* de Victor Hugo. *RHLF* 43: 386-396, juillet-septembre 1936.

Points out similarities of conception and expression between these poems. Cf. Hunt, n. 309.

280. BAUER, H. F. Les *Ballades* de V. Hugo. Leurs origines françaises et étrangères. Champion, 1936. 199 p.

After brief discussion of the manuscript, B. finds that V. H.'s predecessors in France were Millevoye and specially Nodier, and abroad the Germans (Gœthe, Burger, Schiller, and the English (Scott, Moore, Campbell). Also gives information on the composition and reception of the ballads.
Review: F. Michaux in *Bulletin du bibliophile et du bibliothécaire,* n. s. 15ᵉ année; 513-517, 1936.

281. BÉGUIN, A. Le *Songe* de Jean-Paul et Victor Hugo. *RLC* 14: 703-713, oct-déc 1934.

Excellent article on influence of Jean-Paul Richter's poem (particularly the image of the «orbite vide») on V. H. in the *Contemplations* and *Dieu.* Cf. Temple-Patterson, nos. 217-218.

282. BERRET, P. La *Légende des siècles* de Victor Hugo. Étude et analyse. (Collection des chefs-d'œuvre de la littérature expliqués) Mellottée, 1935. 308 p.

Convenient summary of much of the erudition of his critical edition.

283. ——. Le Moyen Age dans la *Légende des siècles* et les sources de V. Hugo. Paulin, 1911. 444 p.

Much of this publication passed into B's critical edition; still useful if critical edition is not available.

284. BISSON, L. A. A Note on the Genesis of «Tristese d'Olympio», stanzas XXXIII & XXXIV, lines 145-149. *FS* 2: 153-155, April 1948.

Source of famous *histrions* metaphor found in a «chose vue» reported by V. H. in *France et Belgique*.

285. BOUCHET, A. du L'Infini et l'inachevé. Victor Hugo. *Cr* 7(2): 946-956, nov 1951.

Discusses *Océan* and *Pierres*.

286. BOUNOURE, G. Abîmes de Victor Hugo. *Mesures* 2: 35-51, 15 juillet 1936.

Suggestive article on the cosmic element in V. H.'s work. Cf. M. Raymond, no. 199.

287. BRUNET, G. Victor Hugo au travail. La composition de «Cérigo». *RHLF* 36: 260-267, avril-juin, 1929.

Valuable study which permits one to follow composition of this poem step by step. It adds to work of Vianey (no. 22) who failed to decipher part of the manuscript. Se also Maury, no. 325.

288. CELLIER, L. Autour des *Contemplations*: George Sand et Victor Hugo. *Archives des lettres modernes*, no. 44, 1962. 35 p.

Includes (1) text of several letters between V. H. and George Sand, (2) her views on the *Contemplations* expressed in two articles in a series «Autour de la table» published in *La Presse*. The second article (June 10, 1856) is reproduced virtually *in extenso*.

289. CHABOSEAU, A. See no. 160.

290. CLANCIER, G. E. Notes sur la poétique de l'œil chez Hugo. *CDS* 54: 87-96, oct-nov 1962.

This good article insists, like several others, on visionary quality of V. H.'s poetry after 1850. Claims that V. H. was naturally a *voyant*, and goes on to assert that in his work there is no more «essential, obsessive, and fascinating image than that of the eye.»

291. CLAUDEL, P. Digression sur Victor Hugo. In his *Positions et propositions*, Vol. I, 39-54. Gallimard, 1928.

Suggestive article on V. H. as a «voyant.» Also maintains that V. H. was essentially an «esprit tourmenté.»

292. COLLIGNON, A. Victor Hugo et Juvénal. *RHLF* 16: 259-284, avril-juin 1909.

Lists numerous reminiscences of Juvenal in V. H.'s work and suggests that «des affinités de génie» explain them.

293. CONSTANS, CH. Victor Hugo poète de l'amour. Béziers, Rodriguez, 1931. 161 p.

Combats opinion that V. H. was not a great love poet, admitting nevertheless that theme of love is less important than others in his work.

294. COUSIN, J. La Préface du recueil *les Rayons et les ombres*. *RHLF* 39: 178-189, janv-mars 1932.

Good analysis of V. H.'s concept of lyric poetry to 1840.

295. DELAFARGE, P. Paris dans la poésie romantique... Victor Hugo, poète de Paris. *RCC* (2e série): 494-506, 30 juin 1934; 630-639, 15 juillet 1934.

Good analysis of this theme in V. H.'s poetry.

296. FLUTRE, F. Éclaircissements sur les *Feuilles d'automne*. *RHLF* 34: 38-71, 403-425, 545-566, 1927.

Explains many allusions in the poems. Cf. Bisson, no. 25.

297. FOURCASSIÉ, J. Sur les sources des poèmes pyrénéens de Victor Hugo. *RHLF* 42: 232-242, avril-juin 1935.

Ingenious article which corrects Berret on a number of points.

298. FRÉMINET, E. Les Sources grecques des «Trois cents». Pp. 1-40 in *Mél. d'histoire littéraire*. (Bibl. de la Faculté des lettres, Univ. de Paris, t. 21) Alcan, 1906.

Chief source is 7th book of Herodotus adapted by V. H. in his own epico-lyric style.

299. GIFFORD, G. H. Hugo's «Pleine mer» and the Great Eastern. *PMLA* 45: 1193-1201, Dec. 1930.

Explains why the steamship is in this poem a symbol of darkness.

300. GLAUSER, A. Victor Hugo et la poésie pure. Geneva, Droz, 1957. 132 p.

Using almost exclusively poems written after 1850 and delving into the very nature of the poetical process, G. maintains that V. H.'s poetry is essentially that of a man possessing extraordinary verbal genius and unusual creative powers, rather than a penetrating intellect or logic. A visionary and a singer, V. H.'s best poetry is «pure poetry.» Some exaggerations and obscurities, but still a stimulating piece of criticism.

Reviews: H. J. Hunt in *FS* 12: 80-81, Jan 1958; M. Maurin in *MLN* 73: 387-390, May 1958; G. Brée in *RR* 49: 150-151, April 1958.

301. GRAMMONT, M. Essai de psychologie linguistique. Style et poésie. Delagrave, 1950. 213 p.

Contains long analyses of «Booz endormi» and «Le Sacre de la Femme» (pp. 15-98).

302. GUIARD, A. La Fonction du poète. Étude sur Victor Hugo. Bloud, 1910; 1926. 316 p.

Standard treatment of this problem of the mission of the poet.

303. GUILLEMIN, H. Vers inédits de Victor Hugo. *CDS* 37e année (no. 300): 189-208, 1950.

Interesting scraps of poetry from V. H.'s papers (presumably preserved in the Bibliothèque Nationale, although G. does not say so.).

304. ──────. Hugo et son poème «Dieu». *Euro* 30: 98-114, fev-mars, 1952.

   Contains some inedita not included in the I. N. edition. See also Journet & Robert, no. 24.

305. GUIMBAUD, L. *Les Orientales* de Victor Hugo. (Collection des Grands Evénements littéraires) Malfère, 1928. 161 p.

   Valuable study of these poems and their sources. See also Barineau, no. 36.
   Review: P. Berret in *RHLF* 39: 133-134, janv.-mars 1932.

306. GUYON, B. La Vocation poétique de Victor Hugo. Essai sur la signification spirituelle des *Odes et ballades* et des *Orientales*. Gap, Impr. Louis-Jean, 1954. 138 p.

   Debatable interpretation.
   Review: J. Pommier in *RHLF* 55: 84-85, janv.-mars 1955.

307. HOFFMANN, L.-F. Autour d'une ode de Victor Hugo: «Le Dévouement». *RR* 55: 91-97, April 1964.

   Article shows that this early ode, inspired by an epidemic in Barcelona in 1821, was treated in generalized fashion by V. H.

308. HOOG, A. Victor Hugo, visionnaire de l'espace. N. Y. The Cultural Division of the French Embassy, 1952. (Planographed brochure) 37 p.

   This lecture presents a valuable interpretation. H. insists on the importance of the table tipping at Jersey and its effects on V. H.'s vision and ideas as revealed in «Ce que dit la bouche d'ombre,» «La Fin de Satan,» and «Dieu.»

309. HUNT, H. J. The Epic in 19th Century France. Oxford, 1941. 446 p.

   Important work in which V. H. looms large. It places V. H.'s epic poetry in proper perspective.
   Reviews: J.-A. Bédé in *RR* 34: 274-279, oct. 1943; J. Voisine in *RHLF* 49: 280-281, juillet-septembre 1949.

310. JACOUBET, H. Sur quelques passages des «Mages». *RHLF* 43: 291-299, juillet-septembre 1936.

Completes and corrects several interpretations in Vianey's critical edition. (no. 22).

311. JAMET, CL. Victor Hugo, poète de l'amour. *RHph* (now *RScH*) n. s. fasc. 25: 47-66, janv-mars 1939.

Underlines V. H.'s «paneroticism» and discusses its place in the poet's philosophy. Debatable conclusion.

312. JASINSKI, R. Sur un poème des *Châtiments*: «L'Art et le peuple». Pp. 397-404 in *Mél. Ed. Huguet*. Boivin, 1940.

Entertaining account of the censorship to which this poem, composed in November 1851, was subjected.

313. JOURNET, R. & G. Robert. Autour des *Contemplations*. Les Belles Lettres, 1955. 192 p. (*Annales littéraires de l'Université de Besançon*, 2e série, t. II., fasc. 6).

Treats three topics: I. Hugo revit-il le texte de ses rééditions? II. Plans et ébauches des *Contemplations*. III. «Choses de la Bible.»

314. ―――. Le Manuscrit des *Contemplations*. Les Belles Lettres, 1956. 206 p. (*Annales littéraires de l'Université de Besançon*, 2e série, t. III, fasc. 5).

These two publications contain a mine of accurate information on the *Contemplations*. They complete and correct Vianey's edition on many points. They give more variant readings; they help date the composition of some of the poems more accurately («A Villequier,» for example). The third study of first volume reveals V. H.'s particular interest in the Bible in 1846.

Reviews: (1st vol.) J.-B Barrère in *RHLF* 57: 267-270, avril-juin 1957; 2nd vol.) J.-B. Barrère in *RHLF* 58: 397-399, juillet-septembre 1958.

315. ―――. Notes sur *Les Contemplations*, suivies d'un Index. Les Belles Lettres, 1958. 398 p. (*Annales littéraires de l'Université de Besançon*, v. 21).

This volume, together with the two preceding ones, constitutes a new critical edition (minus the text). It corrects and supplements Vianey's edition which nevertheless remains useful, particularly as the authors refer to it constantly. These three volumes are indispensable for scholarly and critical treatment of the *Contemplations*. The Index (pp. 245-375) of V. H.'s vocabulary in this *recueil* should be of great value to students of poetic language.

Review: M. Riffaterre in *RR* 51: 69-73, Feb. 1960.

316. JOURNET, R. & G. ROBERT. Des *Feuilles d'automne* aux *Rayons et les ombres*. Étude des manuscrits. Les Belles Lettres, 1957. 269 p. (*Annales litteraires de l'Université de Besançon*, v. 19).

Contains an exact description of the manuscripts and all the variant readings. Supplements the I. N. edition. A few generalizations on V. H.'s corrections are attempted in the Appendix.

317. KOYRÉ, A. L'Occultisme et la poésie. *Cr* 1: 120-125, juin 1946.

Using Viatte's book (no. 226) K. concludes that V. H. composed good poetry with bad metaphysics.

318. KRAPPE, A. H. Note sur Victor Hugo: «Après la bataille». *RHLF* 39: 270-272, avril-juin 1932.

Indicates a possible Danish source for this poem.

319. LARROUTIS, M. Essai sur les sources du «Satyre», *RHLF* 58: 324-364, juillet-septembre 1958.

Author finds in Ballanche's *Essais de palingénésie sociale*, Laprade's *Psyché*, and to a lesser extent in Pierre Leroux's writings the possible origin of the central ideas and symbol of this poem. Cf. Vial, no. 350 and Albouy, no. 139.

320. LEBÈGUE, R. La Genèse d'«Écrit sur la vitre d'une fenêtre flamande». Pp. 359-368 in *Mél. J. Vianey*. Les Presses françaises, 1934.

L. shows that poem was inspired by V. H.'s trip to Belgium in 1837.

321. LE DANTEC, Y. G. Victor Hugo poète lyrique. *RDM* 8e série, 27: 658-669, ler juin 1935.

Excellent critical article containing a survey of V. H.'s various *recueils* with a brief characterization of each one, and with an occasional poem singled out for special comment. A good reply to hostile criticism.

322. LEVAILLANT, M. Dans l'atelier de Victor Hugo. *RDM* 7e série 57: 162-189, ler mai 1930.

In well written article L. discusses some of the initial stages in some of V. H.'s poems, in particular, «A Villequier.»

323. LEVAILLANT, M. Victor Hugo, Juliette Drouet et «Tristesse d'Olympio». See no. 187.

324. MAURIN, M. La Poésie de Victor Hugo et le silence. *Symp* 9: 133-140, Spring, 1955.

Brief but suggestive article on the rôles of sound and silence in V. H.'s poetry.

325. MAURY, P. Cérigo ou un épisode de l'hellénisme en France. *MerF* 183: 392-400, 10 oct 1925.

Author finds the source of this poem in Baudelaire and Nerval. Cf. Brunet, no. 287.

326. MOREAU, P. *Les Contemplations* ou le temps retrouvé. *Archives des lettres modernes* (no. 41) 1962. 62 p.

Author defines contemplation as a superior type of vision and meditation. He views V. H.'s *recueil* as «le livre du souvenir» with 1843 as its focal point. Contains a very subtle and suggestive analysis.

327. ―――. Paysages introspectifs chez Victor Hugo, in *Hommage à Victor Hugo* (pp. 9-25), Strasbourg, 1962.

M. lists and comments on the various images of the human cranium in *Les Contemplations*. He concludes that «le monde introspectif reste un monde intérieur, même si la nature, ses formes, ses couleurs, ses lumières, ses mouvements l'envahissent.»

328. MOUQUET, J. Baudelaire et Victor Hugo en 1842-1843. *MerF* 224: 560-576, 15 déc 1930.

Article on B's dislike of V. H. Speculative rather than authoritative.

329. PÉGUY, CH. Victor-Marie, comte Hugo. Pp. 396-515 in v. 4, *Œuvres complètes*, N. R. F., 1916. 515 p. But the discussion of V. H. really begins in an earlier section entitled «Solvuntur objecta».

Reprint of one of P's *Cahiers de la quinzaine*. Not a biography, but a rambling, subjective criticism of V. H.'s poetry. Interesting.

330. PEYRE, H. Présence de Victor Hugo. Pp. 229-253 in his *Hommes et œuvres du vingtième siècle*. Corrêa, 1938.

Good critical article emphasizing V. H.'s greatness as the poet of the mystery of life.

331. PRUNER, F. *Les Contemplations* «pyramide-temple», ébauche pour un principe d'explication. *Archives des lettres modernes* (no. 43) 1962. 36 p.

Author argues that the *recueil* is, in V. H.'s own words, a «pyramide au dehors, une voûte au-dedans.» V. H., in carrying out this intention created a «chef-d'œuvre d'architecture sacrée.» Ingenious hypothesis ingeniously worked out. Whether it is valid or not is another question.

332. PY, A. Les Mythes grecs dans la poésie de Victor Hugo. Geneva, Droz, 1963. 296 p. (Publications romanes et françaises, v. 76).

Author studies the influence of the Greek myths on V. H., his knowledge of them, his reaction to them, his re-creation of them. P. concludes that V. H.'s vision «spontanément personnifiante et animante a fait naître par son seul exercice, des êtres surnaturels et souvent les a mis aux prises dans des affrontements hésiodiques,» that «d'instinct [...] il est allé de la fable au symbole, du conte au *hieros logos,* du plaisant au sacré; en un mot, de la mythologie au mythe.» Book needs to be read in conjunction with Barrère (nos. 251-253) and Albouy (no. 139).
Reviews: H. J. Hunt in *FS* 19: 75-77, Jan. 1965; P. Albouy in *RHLF* 64: 316-318, avril-juin 1964.

333. RAYMOND, M. See no. 199.

334. RENOUVIER, CH. Victor Hugo, le poète. A. Colin, 1893. 374 p.

Outdated in many respects, but still interesting.

335. RIFFATERRE, M. Victor Hugo's Poetics. *American Society Legion of Honor Magazine* 32(3): 181-196, 1961.

Based on V. H.'s *William Shakespeare* and *Post-scriptum de ma vie,* this article skilfully analyzes V. H.'s conception of the poet as a man who sees beyond reality and records his visions.

336. RIGAL, E. Victor Hugo, poète épique. Société française d'imprimerie et de librairie, 1900. 332 p.

Still useful book, though naturally to be read in conjunction with Berret and Hunt, nos. 28 & 309.

337. ———. Comment ont été composés «Aymerillot» et «Le Mariage de Roland». *RHLF* 7: 1-31, janv-mars 1900.

Excellent study of sources and composition of these poems.

338. ———. Victor Hugo et Byron. *RHLF* 14: 455-461, juillet-septembre 1907.

R. suggests Byronic influence on «L'Expiation» and «La Vision du Dante.» Cf. Berret, no. 19.

339. RINSLER, N. Victor Hugo and the *Poésies allemandes* of Gérard de Nerval. *RLC* 39: 382-395, juillet-septembre 1965.

Author argues persuasively that ideas, themes, and images used by V. H. in *Les Feuilles d'automne* may well have been suggested by Gérard de Nerval's translations of German poets, in particular, Schiller and Gœthe.

340. ROBERT, G. Les Variantes manuscrites de six poèmes des *Chants du crépuscule*. *Annales littéraires de l'Université de Besançon* 3: 33-48, 1953.

Treats «Prélude,» «Dicté après juillet 1830,» «A la Colonne,» «A M. le D. d'O.» «A Louis B.,» «Dans l'église de ***.» A thorough study of this special problem.

341. SCHNEIDER, P. Victor Hugo. *TMod* 6(2): 1761-1793, avril 1951.

Analysis of V. H. as the «poète-océan,» or what the young 20th century littérateur sees in V. H. Interesting.

342. SEEBACHER, J. Sens et structure des «Mages» (*Contemplations*, VI, xxiii). *RScH*, n. s. fasc. 111: 347-370, juillet-septembre 1963.

After a technical examination of the manuscript, S. concludes that the structure of «Les Mages» remained faithful during a complex evolution to the original «symétries,» that these symmetries are organized in relation to a dramatic progression the aim of which is the conquest of what he calls a boundless «espace unitaire.»

343. SOUCHON, P. Quelle fut l'inspiratrice de «La Fête chez Thérèse». *MerF* 291: 554-564, ler mai 1939.

S. argues plausibly that Mme Biard was not the inspiration of this poem.

344. STAPFER, P. Victor Hugo et la grande poésie satirique en France. Ollendorff, 1901. 349 p.

V. H.'s satirical poetry remains intensely lyrical for Stapfer who analyzes V. H.'s satires and compares him to Agrippa d'Aubigné.

345. TEMPLE-PATTERSON, H. Remarques linguistiques sur quatre poèmes de Victor Hugo. *FMod* 23(2): 105-122, avril 1955.

Shows influence of L.-S Mercier's *Néologie* on «Réponse à un acte d'accusation,» «Suite,» «Écrit en 1846,» and «Quelques mots à un autre.» Cf. no. 218.

346. ———. New Light on dark Genius. The Influence of Louis-Sébastien Mercier on the *Contemplations* of Victor Hugo. *MLR* 43: 471-482, July 1948.

Good preliminary study. See no. 218.

347. THOUVENIN, G. Le Symbolisme chez Victor Hugo: le «Cèdre» de la *Légende des siècles*. *RHLF* 47: 147-165, avril-juin 1947.

Interesting interpretation of this poem with further evidence of V. H.'s interest in the Orient and his erudition.

348. ———. See no. 485.

349. UITTI, K. D. The Vision of Lilith in Hugo's *La Fin de Satan*. *FR* 31: 479-486, May 1958.

Author shows that V. H.'s conception of Lilith differs markedly from the cabbalistic legend. While she is the incarnation of evil, she ultimately disappears before the light of Liberté. This sequence corresponds to V. H.'s belief in the progress of humanity «in its struggle for liberation from slavery and for freedom in a peaceful world purged of the scourge of evil.»

350. VIAL, A. Un beau mythe de la *Légende des siècles*: «Le Satyre». *RScH* n. s. fasc. 87: 299-317, juillet-septembre 1957.

Analyzes the text to show that the poem contains a «philosophy of insurrection,» particularly in its affirmation of the virtue and efficacy that Man will give to the universal, cosmic insurrection. As the 16th century placed progress *by* man in opposition to the Christian notion of malediction laid *on* man by original sin, the author sees in this contrast a justification for V. H. to place the poem in that period. The article helps to define the significance of this poem in the *Légende des siècles* and in V. H.'s work in general.

351. VIANEY, J. La Bible dans le lyrisme de Victor Hugo. *RCC* 24e année, 1ère série: 212-228, 15 janv. 1923.

352. ———. La Bible dans la poésie épique de Victor Hugo. *Ibid*. 305-319, 30 jan 1923.

These two articles form a part of Vianey's course on «La Bible dans la poésie française depuis Marot.» They rely heavily on Grillet (no. 498), Convenient.

353. VIATTE, A. Notes sur les sources de Victor Hugo. *RHLF* 39: 434-443, juillet-septembre 1932.

Indicates possible sources for «Ce que dit la bouche d'ombre» and «La Fin de Satan.»

354. ———. Le Mysticisme de Victor Hugo d'après *Océan*. *CDS* (no. 301), 31: 457-467, 1950.

Author sees in *Océan* a confirmation of his earlier thesis (no. 226).

355. WILSON, N. Charles Nodier, Victor Hugo and *Les Feuilles d'automne*. *MLR* 60: 21-31, Jan. 1965.

Author argues with some plausibility that V. H.'s relative silence on political questions in this *recueil* is «intimately related» to his friendship with Charles Nodier.

356. ZUMTHOR, P. Victor Hugo, poète de Satan. Laffont, 1946. 338 p.

Full of ideas, some very debatable, but always stimulating.
Review: H. Guillemin in *Fontaine* 11: 492-493, 1947.

X. THE NOVEL

357. ABRAHAM, P. ET AL. Articles commemorating the Centenary of *Les Misérables*. *Euro* 40: 3-209, février-mars 1962.

Numerous articles of varied value and interest, but those of Ricatte («Dialogue et psychologie»), Albouy («Des hommes, des bêtes et des anges»), Seebacher («Evêques et conventionnels»), Tersen («Le Paris des *Misérables*»), and Milhaud («De l'histoire au roman») are particularly interesting.

358. ALBOUY, P. La «Préface philosophique» des *Misérables* in *Hommage à Victor Hugo*: 103-116. Strasbourg, 1962.

Albouy argues persuasively that the «Préface philosophique» shows that V. H. believed there was no incompatibility between democracy and religion. It indicates, too, that V. H. meant his novel to be «une gigantesque preuve de Dieu et de l'âme.» Cf. no. 357.

359. ANDRÉ, L. Le vrai Claude Gueux. *RPar* 20(5): 89-105, septembre-oct. 1913.

Deals with historical facts behind this «roman à thèse.» Cf. Savey-Casard, no. 20.

360. ANGRAND, P. A propos des *Misérables*: genèse et fortune du roman. *RHLF* 60: 334-344, juillet-septembre 1960.

In some respects article is a review of Guyard's edition (no. 31), but it also gives details not found in that edition, and is particularly useful on the «fortune» of the novel, showing clearly how controversial it seemed in 1862.

361. ———. Javert jaugé, jugé. *MerF* 344: 815-838, avril 1962.

Interesting review of critical reaction in 1862, and an analysis of the opposing points of view.

362. AUBRÉE, E. La Tourgue de Victor Hugo dans la forêt de Fougères. Champion, 1930. 100 p. (Republished under title of *Victor Hugo et Juliette Drouet à Fougères*, Perrin, 1942).

Demonstrates that «la Tourgue,» the medieval tower of *Quatre-vingt-treize*, is the «tour Mélusine» of the Château de Fougères, transported by V. H.'s imagination to the forest.

363. BACH, M. Critique et politique: la réception des *Misérables* en 1862. *PMLA* 77: 595-608, Dec. 1962.

Good survey of the attitudes of critics of all shades of opinion toward V. H.'s novel. Cf. Angrand, no. 360.

364. ――――. Le Vieux Paris dans *Notre-Dame*: sources et ressources de Victor Hugo. *PMLA* 80: 321-324, Sept. 1965.

Good research article proving that one of the principal sources for V. H.'s description of medieval Paris was the «Plan dit de Tapisserie exécutée par Gagnières,» copied in the 19th century (1818) by A. de Mauperché.

365. ――――. The Reception of V. Hugo's First Novels. *Symp* 18: 142-155, Summer 1964.

Good survey of this question: particularly interesting on *Notre-Dame de Paris*.

366. BANASEVIC, N. Les Échos balzaciens dans *Les Misérables* de Victor Hugo in *Hommage à Victor Hugo*: 117-126. Strasbourg, 1962.

Author gives evidence of «echoes» from *Splendeurs et misères des courtisanes, Le Père Goriot, Le Contrat de mariage,* and others.

367. BARBERRY, B. L'Évêque et le conventionnel des *Misérables*. *MerF* 260: 449-473, 15 juin 1935.

B. claims that the old Conventionnel was a man named Sergent and that the well-known scene of the novel had its source in reality.

368. BARRÈRE, J.-B. La Révision des *Misérables* d'après un carnet inédit de Victor Hugo. *RHLF* 62: 555-564, oct-déc 1962.

Examples given by B. throw much light on V. H.'s methods of composition and help to «équilibrer dans une juste appréciation la part de ses traits de geniale imagination et celle du patient métier d'écrivain.» Cf. no. 17.

369. ――――. Observations sur la conception religieuse des *Misérables* in *Hommage à Victor Hugo*: 161-174. Strasbourg, 1962.

Good analysis. The conclusion, perhaps not surprising, is that V. H. was not only profoundly religious, but Christian in the sense that he was a disciple of Christ though not of the priests.

370. BENOIT-LÉVY, E. *Les Misérables* de Victor Hugo. Malfère, 1929. 164 p. (Collection des Grands Événements littéraires).

Not a really complete study, but useful as far as it goes.

371. BERRET, P. Les Comprachicos et la mutilation de Gwynplaine dans *L'Homme qui rit*. *RHLF* 21: 503-518, juillet-déc. 1914.

Shows how V. H.'s imagination, stimulated by recollections of his reading and his travels, transformed gypsies and bandits into the organization of the Comprachicos and attributed to them the mutilation of his hero.

372. ———. Comment Victor Hugo prépara son roman historique de *Quatre-vingt-treize*. *RU* 23(1): 136-145, 15 fév 1914.

B. lists some of the works on the French Revolution at Hauteville House, and indicates briefly those used by V. H. in writing his novel.

373. BUTOR, M. Victor Hugo romancier. *Tel quel* V: 60-77, Hiver 1964.

Original, suggestive interpretation of the structure of V. H.'s major novels.

374. CARLSON, M. L'Art du romancier dans *Les Travailleurs de la mer* (les techniques visuelles de Hugo). *Archives des lettres modernes* (no. 38) 1961. 55 p.

Author says some accurate and interesting things about the novel and the effects created by V. H., but does not really come to grips with the technical problems of style.

375. CELLIER, L. «Chaos vaincu». Victor Hugo et le roman initiatique in *Hommage à Victor Hugo*: 213-223. Strasbourg, 1962.

Interesting article in which C. defines the «roman initiatique» as a work in which a human soul is subjected to a series of ordeals and ends by reaching a superior stage of development. He sees in «Chaos vaincu» the pivot of *L'Homme qui rit*: what precedes is the «petite initiation»; what follows is the «grande initiation.» Gwynplaine's suicide is not a negative but a positive thing. His smile at the end is the «sourire de l'Initié.»

376. CHARLIER, G. Comment fut écrit *Le Dernier Jour d'un condamné*. *RHLF* 22: 321-360, juillet-déc. 1915.

Authoritative study of the genesis, sources, and composition of this work.

377. COUSIN, J. Mgr Myriel dans les *Misérables*. *RHLF* 33: 420-426, juillet-septembre 1926.

Fact and fiction in V. H.'s portrayal of the Bishop.

378. DEBIEN, G. Un roman colonial de Victor Hugo: *Bug Jargal*, ses sources et ses intentions historiques. *RHLF* 52: 298-313, juillet-septembre 1952.

Authoritative article showing that in its final form *Bug Jargal* owes more to documentary than to oral sources, and that the theme of anti-slavery is amplified by the more general problem of colored versus white.

379. DROUET, JULIETTE. Souvenirs du couvent. *RHLF* 62: 523-533, oct-déc 1962.

A reproduction of a ms. preserved in the Bibliothèque Nationale. The information was used by V. H. in composing the well-known episode of Le Petit-Picpus in *Les Misérables*. Cf. below, Pommier, no. 414.

380. DUMESNIL, R. L'Origine de deux livres des *Misérables*. *MerF* 91: 77-93, ler mai 1911.

Le Cloître Saint-Méry by Rey-Dusseuil is an important source of «L'Idylle rue Plumet» and «L'Épisode rue Saint-Denis.»

381. GAUDON, J. «Je ne sais quel jour de soupirail» (automne 1845 printemps 1847) in *Hommage à Victor Hugo*: 149-160. Strasbourg, 1962.

G. argues that the first version of the novel, i. e. *Les Misères*, points already by its coloration and its themes to the great poetry and prose of later years.

382. GAULMIER, J. De Fantine aux Vaudois d'Arras in *Hommage à Victor Hugo*: 85-94. Strasbourg, 1962.

This contribution has a twofold interest: 1) G. finds the source of Fantine in Muston's *Histoire complète des Vaudois du Piémont*, 1843; 2) the fact that *vaudois* was synonymous with *sorcier* may have suggested to V. H. the accusation of sorcery brought against Esmeralda in *Notre-Dame de Paris*.

383. GELY, C. Baudelaire et Victor Hugo: influences réciproques. *RHLF* 62: 592-595, oct-déc 1962.

G. suggests that V. H. found the name of Éponine in B's «Petites vieilles.» He also suggests that the vision of a ragged, young girl mentioned in the *V. H. raconté* may be the origin of the tragic figure of Éponine.

384. GEORGEL, P. Vision et imagination plastique dans *Quatre-vingt-treize*. *Les Lettres romanes* XIX: 3-27, fév. 1965.

Author suggests that V. H. distinguished three different moments (*temps*) of poetic activity: observation, imagination, intuition. He examines passages of *Quatre-vingt-treize* from these points of view. Interesting article, particularly in its comments on V. H.'s depiction of La Tourgue.

385. GIRARD, R. Monstres et demi-dieux dans l'œuvre de Hugo. *Symp* XIX: 50-57, spring 1965.

Article is centered on the hero of *L'Homme qui rit*; points out that V. H. identified himself with his man-made monster, and develops the notion that «toutes les relations humaines, dans *L'Homme qui rit*, sont symbolisées par la mutilation.» Interesting article, though here and there debatable.

386. GIRAUD, J. Victor Hugo et le *Monde* de Rocoles. *RHLF* 17: 497-530, juillet-septembre 1910.

Judicious study of V. H.'s use of this book in «La Légende du beau Pécopin.»

387. GUSDORF, G. «Quel horizon on voit du haut de la barricade» in *Hommage à Victor Hugo*: 175-196. Strasbourg, 1962.

Author shows in some detail that Enjolras' speech is central to the ideology of *Les Misérables* and that it is typical of those whom he calls the «révolutionnaires du xixe siècle français.»

388. GUYARD, M.-F. «Creuser Mabeuf» in *Hommage à Victor Hugo*: 95-102. Strasbourg, 1962.

V. H.'s additions, in the course of composing the novel, indicate that he intended to give Mabeuf constantly greater significance.

389. HUARD, G. *Notre-Dame de Paris* et les antiquaires de Normandie. *RHLF* 53: 319-344, juillet-septembre 1953.

H. demonstrates that V. H. owed much, although sometimes indirectly, to the Norman antiquaries, Caumont, Le Prévost, Langlois, and others.

390. HUARD, G. Le Petit-Picpus des *Misérables* et les informatrices de Victor Hugo: Mme Biard et Juliette Drouet. *RHLF* 60: 345-387, juillet-septembre 1960.

Article supersedes that of Le Breton (no. 397) H. demonstrates that V. H.'s information came not only from Juliette Drouet but also from Mme Biard and from documentary sources (e. g. Sauval and Moreri). See also Pommier, no. 414.

391. HUGUET, E. Quelques sources de *Notre-Dame de Paris*. *RHLF* 8: 48-79; 425-455; 622-649; 1901.

Important study of sources showing V. H.'s debt to Sauval, Jehan de Troyes, Commynes, P. Mathieu, Du Breul, and Collin de Plancy.

392. HUNT, H. J. Le Sens épique des *Misérables* in *Hommage à Victor Hugo*: 127-138. Strasbourg, 1962.

Author makes a skilful comparison of the novel and the *Légende des siècles*, finding many points of similarity, above all, an identical philosophy of history and a humanitarian «mystique.»

393. JOURNET, R. & G. ROBERT. A propos du Reliquat des *Misérables*: le classement des papiers de Hugo à la Bibliothèque Nationale in *Hommage à Victor Hugo*: 39-49. Strasbourg, 1962.

A highly technical (and able) report on the disorder existing in the arrangement of many of the papers left by V. H., particularly the fragmentary ones. See also no. 394.

394. ———. Le Manuscrit des *Misérables*. (*Annales de l'Université de Besançon*, v. 61). Les Belles Lettres, 1963.

Technical, able presentation, containing a «chronologie sommaire,» complete variant readings for 83 chapters, and for others V. H.'s additions. There is also a summary of the modifications of the names of characters.
Review: J. Seebacher in *RHLF* 65: 518-521, juillet-septembre 1965.

395. ———. Le Mythe du peuple dans *Les Misérables*. Éditions sociales, 1964. 214 p.

Devotes one chapter to works before *Les Misères;* two to *Les Misères;* four to *Les Misérables*. Defines a myth as «une belle et émouvante histoire,

simple en somme, qui projette devant l'homme l'image de son destin.» Concludes that for V. H. the people have a collective soul which will lead them from darkness into light. A thorough-going analysis of this subject.
Review: J. Seebacher in *RHLF* 65: 518-521, juillet-septembre 1965.

396. LARROUTIS, M. J. de Maistre et Victor Hugo: le bourreau dans *Han d'Islande*. *RHLF* 62: 573-575, oct-déc 1962.

V. H. borrowed from de Maistre the notion of the solitude of the executioner, avoided by his fellow men.

397. LE BRETON, A. Réalité et fiction. Le vrai Petit-Picpus des *Misérables*. *RDM* 7e série, v. 28: 313-340, 15 juillet 1925.

Analyzes the mingling of truth and fiction in V. H.'s description. See Huard, no. 389 and Pommier, no. 414.

398. LEUILLIOT, B. Présentation de Jean Valjean in *Hommage à Victor Hugo*: 51-68. Strasbourg, 1962.

L. sees in Jean Valjean a sort of demonstration or realization of the «puissance de rêve,» characteristic of certain creations of V. H. He also, more debatably, makes a close rapprochement between J. V. and John of Patmos.

399. MACLEAN, C. M. Victor Hugo's Use of *Les Délices de la Grande Bretagne* in *L'Homme qui rit*. *MLR* 8: 173-184, April 1913.

400. ———. Victor Hugo's Use of Chamberlayne's *L'État présent de l'Angleterre*. *MLR* 8: 496-510, Oct. 1913.

Useful source studies, perhaps not as thorough as possible, showing how V. H. used the first book (*Les Délices...*) for local color, the second (*L'État present...*) for factual information which would serve the political and social ideas he wished to emphasize.

401. MAIGRON, L. Le Roman historique à l'époque romantique. Essai sur l'influence de Walter Scott. Hachette, 1898. 443 p.

Contains a still valuable discussion of *Notre-Dame de Paris*.

402. MESSAC, R. Autour de Gavroche. *RHLF* 35: 577-589, oct-déc 1928.

Finds the source of Gavroche and his *milieu* in Eugène Sue, Ponson du Terrail, and others.

403. MILHAUD, G. See no. 357.

404. MOORE, O. H. The Sources of Victor Hugo's *Quatre-vingt-treize*. PMLA 39: 368-405, June 1924.

405. ———. Further Sources of Victor Hugo's *Quatre-vingt-treize*. PMLA 41: 452-461, June 1926.

These two articles show V. H.'s indebtedness to Louis Blanc, Lamartine, Mercier, and others. Cf. F. Page, no. 408 and H. Temple-Patterson, no. 218.

406. ———. How Victor Hugo created the Characters of *Notre-Dame de Paris*. PMLA 57: 255-274, March 1942.

M. studies the manuscripts to show how the leading characters evolved.

407. ———. Realism in *Les Misérables*. PMLA 61: 211-228, March 1946.

Interesting article on some of V. H.'s documentation and his increasing tendency toward accuracy.

408. PAGE, F. Une source de Victor Hugo: *Quatre-vingt-treize*. MLR 14, 183-193, April 1919.

Author finds that many picturesque details of revolutionary Paris come from L.-S. Mercier. Cf. H. Temple-Patterson, no. 218.

409. PÉÈS, S. L'Origine de la couleur locale scandinave dans le *Han d'Islande* de Victor Hugo. RLC 9: 261-284, avril-juin 1929.

Good study of sources for historical and geographical details of this novel.

410. PHILIPOT, E. Étienne Binet et Victor Hugo. RHLF 16: 88-109, janv-mars 1909.

Finds source of several passages of «Le Beau Pécopin» (*Le Rhin*) in Binet's *Essay des Merveilles de Nature*.

411. PIROUÉ, G. Victor Hugo romancier ou les dessous de l'inconnu. Denoël, 1964. 252 p.

Interesting and original ideas on V. H.'s novels. Some of P.'s views are highly debatable, but always stimulating.

412. POMMIER, J. L'Histoire des *Misérables*. *La Revue (des Deux Mondes)* 19: 339-353, 1er oct 1962.

Excellent summary of the composition of the novel from its earliest conception to its publication.

413. ——. Premiers pas dans l'étude des *Misérables* in *Hommage à Victor Hugo*: 29-37. Strasbourg, 1962.

P. calls attention (1) to the unreliability of G. Simon's edition of *Les Misères*, (2) to certain errors in the «Historique» of the I. N. edition of *Les Misérables*. He also suggests the possibility of various sources such as Paul de Kock and Jules Janin.

414. ——. Sur *les Misérables*: I. La Relation de Juliette. II. Un pseudo-modèle de Jean Valjean. III. Le portrait de Marius. *RHLF* 62: 534-554, oct-déc 1962.

P. discusses in I Juliette's text in relation to V. H.'s novel, completing and correcting G. Huard (no. 390). In II he successfully challenges the belief that the model for J. V. was one Pierre Maurin. In III he establishes that the portrait of Marius in the novel is not a complete self-portrait of V. H.

415. REMIGEREAU, F. Pour une mise au point: Du Fouilloux, E Binet, Rocoles et Victor Hugo. *RHLF* 40: 513-537, oct-déc 1933; 41: 32-53, janv-mars 1934.

Source study for «Le Beau Pécopin» (*Le Rhin*).
Cf. nos. 75, 410, 497.

416. RICATTE, R. Sur *les Misérables*. Le moraliste et ses personnages. *MerF* 342: 48-65, 1er mai 1961.

R. argues persuasively that V. H.'s aim was less to analyze or portray human nature than to change it, and that what psychology there is in the novel is sensorial rather than analytical.

417. ——. Style parlé et psychologie dans *les Misérables* in *Hommage à Victor Hugo*: 139-147. Strasbourg, 1962.

R. shows how the spoken word supports psychological presentation, and at least in one case, that of Gavroche, is all important. Cf. no. 357.

418. Roos, J. Le Thème de la régénération dans *les Misérables* in *Hommage à Victor Hugo*: 197-205, 1962.

Points out what is fairly obvious that redemption is accomplished in the novel by suffering, humility, education, and example.

419. SAURAT, D. *Les Misérables. Euro* 30: 134-138, fév-mars 1952.

Brief but suggestive criticism.

420. SEEBACHER, J. La Mort de Jean Valjean in *Hommage à Victor Hugo*: 69-84. Strasbourg, 1962.

Compares the death of J. V. with that of Goriot, then analyzes the text in the light of V. H.'s philosophy. Makes effective use of V. H.'s marginal additions.

421. ———. See no. 357.

422. ———. En marge des *Misérables*. I. Le bonhomme Royol et son cabinet de lecture. II. Victor Hugo héritier de sa tante Martin-Chopine. *RHLF* 62: 575-592, oct-déc 1962.

In I Seebacher gives interesting facts on Royol, the friend of Mabeuf. In II he speculates on the source of the «flambeaux d'argent massif» owned by Mgr Myriel.

423. SIMAÏKA, R. L'Inspiration épique dans les romans de Victor Hugo. Minard, 1962. 232 p.

S. distinguishes between the *romans dramatiques* and the *romans épiques* of V. H. Book contains comments many of which are not very new, others which are either not wholly clear or debatable.
Reviews: O. H. Moore in *FR* 37: 245-246, Dec. 1963; J. Seebacher in *RHLF* 63: 684, oct-déc. 1963; H. J. Hunt in *FS* 18: 69-70, Jan. 1964.

424. SIMON, G. Victor Hugo: *Les Misères*. See no. 33.

425. SOURIAU, M. Le Concours de grimaces de *Notre-Dame de Paris* et ses sources. *RCC* 10e année, 1ère série: 560-568, 30 janv 1902.

Suggests that an item in Addison's *Spectator* was the original stimulus for this famous scene.

426. TERSEN, E. See no. 357.

XI. Theater

427. ASCOLI, G. *L'Amy Robsart* de Victor Hugo. *RCC* 32e année, 2e série: 289-299 (mai); 501-516 (juin); 1931.

    Careful study of disputed authorship and composition of this early play.

428. BALDENSPERGER, F. Les Années 1827-1828 en France et au dehors. Conclusion. *Cromwell* et sa préface. *RCC* 30e année, 2e série: 528-542, juin 1929.

    Sensitive and judicious treatment of V. H.'s play and preface.

429. BERRET, P. L'Affaire des *Jumeaux* de Victor Hugo. *MerF* 250: 17-27, 15 fév. 1934.

    A sound article on the reasons why V. H. never completed this play.

430. BERTAUT, J. La Première du *Roi s'amuse*. *RDM* 8e série, 12: 431-443, 15 nov 1932.

    Good account of this stormy performance.

431. BLANCHARD, M. *Marie Tudor*. Essai sur les sources du drame. Boivin, 1934. 396 p.

    Good critical study of sources and composition.
    Review: H. Kurz in *RR* 25: 167-169, April 1934.

432. BUTOR, M. Le Théâtre de Victor Hugo. *NRF* 12e année: 862-878 (nov), 1073-1081 (déc), 1964; 13e année: 105-113, janv 1965.

    In these articles B. seeks to show that V. H.'s theater is not subsidiary to the rest of his work, and that it teaches us something «about the very nature of today's theater, about that of the 19th century, and about what separates us from that period».

433. CHARLIER, G. *Hernani* et le *Figaro*. *MerF* 305: 459-465, ler mars 1949.

    Relates the hostility of the *Figaro's* critic (Latouche?) to the play.

434. CITOLEUX, M. Alfred de Vigny, Victor Hugo et *Marion de Lorme*. *RHLF* 35: 439-440, juillet-septembre 1928.

C. links the play with Vigny's *Cinq-Mars*. Cf. Tournier, no. 465.

435. CURZON, H. DE. *Amy Robsart* de Victor Hugo. Le manuscrit pour la représentation (1828). *RHLF* 35: 495-527, oct-déc 1928.

Manuscript for the stage production, discovered in the Archives Nationales, is described, and passages hitherto unpublished are given *in extenso*. Cf. no. 427.

436. DEBIDOUR, A. Une source probable des *Burgraves*. *RHLF* 40: 38-48, janv-mars 1933.

Judicious article on imitation and originality in this play. Cf. Giraud, no. 441, and Russell, no. 461.

437. DRAPER, F. W. M. The Rise and Fall of the French Romantic Drama, with special reference to the influence of Shakespeare, Scott, and Byron. London, Constable, 1923. 303 p.

Contains some good pages on V. H.'s theater.

438. DU BOS, M. Une source inconnue des erreurs historiques du *Roi s'amuse*. *MerF* 240: 23-42, 15 nov. 1932.

Finds the source in Paul Lacroix's novel, *Les Deux Fous* (1830).

439. EVANS, D. O. The Hegelian Idea in *Hernani*. *MLN* 63: 171-173, March 1948.

Brief but interesting article with special comment on Carlos' monologue.

440. GAUDON, J. Victor Hugo dramaturge. L'Arche, 1955. 158 p. (Collection: Les Grands Dramaturges.)

This brief but intelligent book discusses the question whether V. H. succeeded in creating the «théâtre populaire» which he sought to do. It calls attention to certain important features of V. H.'s theater (such as the «nostalgie de la mort»), and emphasizes the rôle of costume and scenery.
Review: H. Temple-Patterson in *MLR* 52: 118-119, Jan 1957.

441. GIRAUD, J. Étude sur quelques sources des *Burgraves*. *RHLF* 16: 501-539, juillet-septembre 1909.

Discriminating article on V. H.'s use of Schreiber, Kohlrausch, Grillparzer, and others. Cf. no. 436, 461.

442. GLACHANT, PAUL & VICTOR. Un laboratoire dramatique. Essai critique sur le théâtre de Victor Hugo. Hachette, 1902-1903. 2 v. 401, 516 p.

Still useful studies of the plays by means of the manuscripts.

443. GUILLOTON, V. *Hernani* et l'honneur castillan. *Smith College Studies in Modern Languages* 21: 103-109, 1939-1940.

G. finds that the standard of honor presented as Spanish in *Hernani* is not different from that displayed by the Frenchman, d'Auverney, in *Bug Jargal*.

444. ISAY, R. Hugo, le dernier Burgrave, ou le secret de Victor Hugo. *La Revue (des Deux Mondes)* 10: 465-489, 1949.

Very debatable interpretation which links the play with «le mirage allemand», Eschylus, the Napoleonic concept, Eugène Hugo's madness and death.

445. LA FORCE, DUC DE. *Lucrèce Borgia,* drame en trois actes ... et en vers de Victor Hugo. *RDM* 8e série 31: 171-179, janv-mars 1936.

Calls attention to existence of many alexandrines in the prose of this play.

446. LAMBERT, F. Le Manuscrit du *Roi s'amuse*. (*Annales littéraires de l'Université de Besançon*, v. 63). Les Belles Lettres, 1964. 127 p.

Contains variant readings, *brouillons*, and preparatory notes (B. N. n. a. f. 13370); also a study (pp. 71-90) of the genesis of the play.
Review: R. Journet in *RHLF* 65: 709, oct-déc. 1965.

447. LANCASTER, H. C. The Genesis of *Ruy Blas*. *MP* 14: 641-646, March 1917.

L. maintains that original idea of the play is found in the situation at the end of the third act.

448. LANSON, G. Victor Hugo et Angelica Kauffmann. *RHLF* 22: 392-401, juillet-décembre 1915.

L. found in the marriage of A. K. with the false Count de Horn one of the principal sources of *Ruy Blas*.

449. LE BRETON, A. Le Théâtre romantique. Boivin, 1926. 250 p.

Still useful for several of V. H.'s plays.

450. LEVAILLANT, M. Un drame inconnu de Victor Hugo in *Mél Daniel Mornet* (pp. 199-208). Nizet, 1951.

Brief but adequate study of *Mille francs de récompense*.

451. ———. Le Premier Ruy Blas et les trois Don César in *Mél J. Vianey* (pp. 369-378). Les Presses françaises, 1934.

Repeats old theory that Ruy Blas' love for the queen was inspired by an episode of Rousseau's *Confessions;* shows that V. H. first thought of Don César about 1830.

452. LOTE, G. En préface à *Hernani*. Cent ans après. Gamber, 1930. 200 p.

Good study as far as it goes, but the problem of play's genesis remains unsolved.

453. LYONNET, H. Les Premières de Victor Hugo. Delagrave, 1930. 234 p.

Lively, entertaining book which relates opening nights not only of V. H.'s principal plays but also of *La Esmeralda* and of plays drawn from his novels. Gives details on distribution of rôles, audience reaction, box office receipts, etc. Includes information on readings of V. H.'s poems at the Théâtre Français.

454. MONTARGIS, J. La Première et la Dernière Œuvre dramatique de Victor Hugo. *NRF* 52: 456-477, 1er mars 1939.

Includes text of *Le Château du diable* (written in 1812) and announces that of *Le Suicide* (1878).

455. MOORE, O. H. How Victor Hugo altered the characters of Don César and Ruy Blas. *PMLA* 47: 827-833, Sept. 1932.

Completes Lanson's article, no. 448.

456. MOREL-FATIO, A. L'Histoire dans *Ruy Blas* in his *Études sur l'Espagne*. Vieweg, 1888.

Examines V. H.'s use of *Mémoires de la cour d'Espagne* and *État présent de l'Espagne* showing the changes V. H. made. Cf. Martinenche, no. 474.

457. PENDELL, W. D. Victor Hugo's Acted Dramas and the Contemporary Press. Baltimore, Johns Hopkins Press, 1947. 135 p.

Useful compilation for this subject.
Review: H. J. Hunt in *MLR* 44: Jan. 1949.

458. PURNAL, R. See no. 42.

459. RIFFATERRE, M. Un exemple de comédie symboliste chez Victor Hugo. *L'Esprit créateur* 5: 162-173, Fall 1965.

Author suggests that in *Mangeront-ils?* (in *Théâtre en liberté*), which he calls symbolist rather than symbolic, the essential theme is the struggle between Good and Evil. He calls attention to V. H.'s use of the comic achieved through irony, parody, etc.

460. RIGAL, E. La Genèse d'un drame romantique, *Ruy Blas*. *RHLF* 20: 753-788, oct-déc 1913.

Study of sources with special emphasis on Gaillardet's *Struensée*. Cf. Lancaster, no. 447 and Lanson, no. 448.

461. RUSSELL, O. W. Étude historique et critique des *Burgraves* de Victor Hugo. Avec variantes inédites et lettres inédites. Nizet, 1962. 280 p.

Fairly detailed doctoral thesis on conception and genesis of this «drame sans limites», indicating that V. H. was already evolving from the lyric poet of the 1830s into the seer he later became. One chapter of criticism and one on the reception of the play.
Reviews: H. J. Hunt in *FS* 18: 281-282, July 1964; M. Riffaterre in *RR* 55: 220-221, Oct. 1964; J. Seebacher in *RHLF* 65: 517-518, juillet-septembre 1965.

462. SÉE, H. Le Cromwell de Victor Hugo et le Cromwell de l'histoire. *MerF* 200: 5-17, 15 septembre 1927.

Maintains that V. H.'s Cromwell has little resemblance to the historical Cromwell.

463. SIMON, G. A propos de *Marion de Lorme*. *RPar* 14 (2): 420-448, mars-avril, 1907.

Interesting commentary with some hitherto unpublished documents.

464. SOURIAU, M. See no. 39.

465. TOURNIER, G. Les Points de départ du *Cromwell* de Victor Hugo. *RLC* 7: 87-110, janv.-mars 1927.

T. links the play not only with Villemain's *Histoire de Cromwell* and other sources listed by V. H. himself, but also with Vigny's *Cinq-Mars*, Scott, and Shakespeare. Cf. no. 434.

466. VIANEY, J. La Légende et l'histoire de Frédéric Barberousse dans *les Burgraves*. *Mémoires de l'Académie des sciences et lettres de Montpellier*, 2e. série, t. 5, no. 2: 49-69, 1909.

V. finds sources in works of Grimm, Pfister, Schmidt, and Pfeffel; considers that in spite of some errors of detail, the character of the hero and the epoch was well understood by V. H. Cf. 441.

XII. FOREIGN INFLUENCES

467. AVÉROFF, G. Victor Hugo et l'indépendance de la Grèce. *RLC* 328-332, avril-juin 1952.

Brief introduction to this subject.
(In this same volume of the *RLC* are found other brief articles on V. H.'s attitude toward various countries).

468. BARRÈRE, J.-B. Victor Hugo et la Grande Bretagne. *RLC* 28: 137-167, avril-juin 1954.

Excellent survey and analysis of this subject, showing (1) that V. H.'s contact with Scott and Shakespeare aided in the development of his own genius, (2) that except for a few of the novels his work was ill appreciated in England, (3) that he shared many of the popular French prejudices about the English. Cf. no. 506; also Hooker and Thomas, nos. 473 & 484.

469. BÉGUIN, A. See no. 281.

470. DÉDÉYAN, Ch. Victor Hugo et l'Allemagne. *AUP* 23: 539-560. oct.-déc. 1953.

A rapid survey of the question, with an analysis of *Le Rhin* and more briefly of *Les Burgraves*, and the Germanic poems of the *Légende des siècles*. D. also shows how the enthusiasm of the 1840s and 1850s was followed by disillusion in 1870 and after.

471. ―――. Victor Hugo et l'Allemagne. 2 vols. Minard, 1964, 1965. 265 p. & 308 p.

First volume runs from 1802 to 1830; second, from 1830 to 1848. Both periods are examined in great detail with a discussion of the possible influence on V. H. of Mme de Staël's book and of Gœthe, Schiller, Lessing, Kotzebue, and others. Valuable treatment of this subject.
Review: Vol. I., A. Monchoux in *RHLF* 65: 709-711, oct-déc. 1965.

472. DRAPER, F. W. M. See no. 437.

473. HOOKER, K. W. The Fortunes of Victor Hugo in England. N. Y. Columbia University Press, 1938. 333 p.

Good book showing that before 1860 V. H.'s work was little known in England, and, even when known, was not well thought of. *Les Misérables* and *Quatre-vingt-treize* finally brought him success with the public if not with the critics. In last period of his life, Swinburne, Dowden, and to some extent Tennyson held him in esteem.
Review: F. C. Green in *MLR* 35: 106-108, Jan. 1940.

474. MARTINENCHE, E. L'Espagne et le romantisme français. Hachette, 1922. 256 p.

Contains an important discussion of V. H.'s use of Spanish themes, allusions, etc. in his poetry and drama.
Review: P. Hazard in *RLC* 3: 172-174, janv-mars 1923.

475. MORAUD, M. Le Romantisme français en Angleterre de 1814 à 1848. Champion, 1933. 479 p.

Authoritative treatment, in spite of some inaccuracies, of this subject which includes, of course, V. H.
Reviews: M. E. I. Robertson in *MLR* 29: 100-101, Jan. 1934; E. Seillière in *RLC* 14: 594-598, juillet-septembre 1934.

476. PARTRIDGE, E. The French Romantics' Knowledge of English Literature 1820-1848. Champion, 1924. 370 p.

V. H. treated among others. Cf. Barrère, no. 468.
Review: C. H. Herford in *MLR* 20: 354-356, July 1925.

477. PIÉTRI, F. L'Espagne de Victor Hugo. I. De *Bug Jargal* aux *Orientales*. La Revue (des Deux Mondes) 22 (no. 16): 601-609, 15 août 1951.

478. ———. II. De *Cromwell* à *Hernani*. *Ibid*. 23 (no. 17): 58-76, 1er. septembre 1951.

479. ———. III. *Ruy Blas*. *Ibid*. 25 (no. 1): 57-77, 1er janv. 1952.

480. ———. IV. La *Légende des siècles*. *Ibid*. 25 (no. 4): 649-672, 15 fév. 1952.

481. ———. V. Les Dernières Œuvres. *Ibid*. 29 (no. 20): 657-671, 15 oct. 1952.

In this series of articles author seeks to prove by a fairly detailed examination of texts that V. H.'s Spain, while fanciful and imaginative, is more accurately depicted than has been often thought. Except for Morel-Fatio (no. 456), P. ignores the work of scholars.

482. RINSLER, N. See no. 339.

483. SCHWAB, R. See no. 214.

484. THOMAS, J. H. L'Angleterre dans l'Œuvre de Victor Hugo. Pedone, 1934. 245 p.

Analyzes V. H.'s treatments of English subjects and his use of English sources; concludes that V. H. and the English temperament were incompatible. Contains a useful bibliography. Cf. Barrère, no. 468.

485. THOUVENIN, G. La Légende orientale de Nemrod et «Le Glaive» de Victor Hugo. *RHLF* 40: 49-76, janv.-mars 1933.

Article, rejecting the opinions of Rigal and Jourda, claims that V. H. found his source in oriental folk-lore, in particular, in Belami's version of the chronicle of Abu-Djafar Mohammed Tabari, translated and edited by Louis Dubeux in 1836.

XIII. MISCELLANEOUS

486. BARRÈRE, J.B. Les livres de Hauteville-House. *RHLF* 51: 441-455, oct.-déc. 1951; 52: 48-72, janv.-mars 1952.

B. classifies the books and concludes they constituted for V. H. «une bibliothèque de travail d'abord, d'occasion ensuite, et enfin de fidélité aux souvenirs, aux amitiés, aux simples relations.» See no. 506; also Delalande, no. 78.

487. BART, B. F. Victor Hugo and the *Journal des artistes*, 1838-1840. *Symp* 4: 397-407, Nov. 1950.

Author gives examples of the hostility of a prominent anti-Romantic editor, Étienne Huard, to V. H.

488. BARTHOU, L. Victor Hugo: Carnets et dessins inédits. *RDM* 6e. série, 48: 721-761, 15 déc. 1918.

Numerous quotations and sketches from V. H.'s note-books of 1856, 1857, 1861, 1871-2, 1877.

489. ———. Autour du *William Shakespeare* de Victor Hugo. Documents inédits. *RPar* 27 (4): 449-486, 1er. août 1920.

Interesting details on the composition and arrangement of this book and on technical matters of printing, publication, publicity, etc.

490. BENDA, J. Victor Hugo et la musique. *RMus* 16: 161-166, septembre-oct. 1935.

Claims that V. H.'s genius and temperament prevented him from loving music (in the purest definition of that expression).

491. BRAUN, S. D. The «Courtisane» in the French Theater from Hugo to Becque (1831-1885). Baltimore, Johns Hopkins Press, 1947. 157 p.

Useful compilation and discussion.
Review: G. B. Fitch in *MLN* 63: 204-205, March 1948.

492. CHESNER DU CHESNE, A. Le *Ronsard* de Victor Hugo. *MerF* 174: 346-371, 1ᵉʳ septembre 1924.

Detailed description of this famous volume in which V. H.'s friends inscribed verses.

493. DAUBRAY, C. Sur le *William Shakespeare* de Victor Hugo. *RFrance* 17 (5): 268-300, 1937.

D. has drawn some interesting items from the *Reliquat* and printed them with her comments.

494. DE BOER, J. P. Chr. Victor Hugo et l'enfant. Nizet & Bartard, 1936. 275 p.

Satisfactory survey of the theme of childhood in V. H.'s work.

495. DRESSE DE LEBIOLES, P. Gœthe et Victor Hugo. Brussels, Ed. Libris, 1942. 179 p.

Comparison of two writers with an attempted explanation of their mutual dislike. Cf. Baldensperger, no. 142.

496. GEORGE, A. Early American Criticism of Victor Hugo. *FR* 11: 287-293, Feb. 1938.

American reactions from 1828 to 1852 were few and mostly hostile.

497. GIRAUD, J. Une source inconnue du *Rhin* de Victor Hugo. *RHLF* 29: 165-191, avril-juin 1922.

Interesting study of V. H.'s use of *Estats, empires et principautez* by Pierre Davity. Cf. Remigereau, no. 415.

498. GRILLET, Cl. La Bible dans Victor Hugo. Hachette, 1910. 350 p.

Useful compilation and thorough study, too speculative perhaps in its conclusions.

499. HAMELIN, J. Les Plaidoiries de V. Hugo. (Préface de Fernand Payen) Hachette, 1935. 126 p.

Gives full text of several of V. H.'s pleas before the courts, preceded by an explanation of each lawsuit. Most important is that of June 11, 1851 in which he defended his son for having attacked the death-penalty.

500. LEY-DEUTSCH, M. Le Gueux chez Victor Hugo. Droz, 1936. 490 p.

Detailed study of the beggar, knave, ragamuffin, convict in V. H.'s novels and plays. Contains useful bibliography.

501. SERGENT, J. Rythme poétique et musique. *RMus* 16: 197-214, septembre-oct. 1935.

Attempts to show that while V. H. was untutored in music, he came to have genuine feeling for it.
Cf. Benda, no. 490.

502. SHORTLIFFE, G. Hugo's Intervention for Henri Rochefort. *Symp* 2: 242-260, November 1948.

Corrects previous writers and shows that V. H.'s efforts to free H. R. failed.

503. TIERSOT, J. Victor Hugo musicien. *RMus* 16: 167-196, septembre-oct. 1935.

Title a misnomer, for the article deals mostly with V. H.'s relations with musicians of his time.

504. VIVIER, M. Hugo et Nodier collaborateurs de «l'Oriflamme.» *RHLF* 58: 297-323, juillet-septembre 1958.

Hitherto unknown chapter in the history of romanticism is contributed by this article which reveals the rôle played by the short-lived paper, *L'Oriflamme*, in the «bataille romantique» and the contributions of V. H., Nodier, and Saint-Valry to it.

ADDENDA

505. BARRÈRE, J.-B. Victor Hugo (Collections des Écrivains devant Dieu). Desclée de Brouwer, 1965. 141 p.

The Introduction (pp. 13-87) is a valuable *mise-au-point* of V. H.'s religious views and beliefs. The rest of the book is an anthology of texts from V. H.'s letters and works treating these questions. Cf. Le Cœur, no. 46.

506. ———. Victor Hugo à l'œuvre: le poète en exil et en voyage. Klincksieck, 1965. 328 p.

Reproduces, with modifications and important additions, previous studies: see nos. 54, 486, 468, 276, 275, 144. Taken together, they shed light on V. H.'s creative genius. Gives in appendices lists of books in Hauteville-House.

507. FONGARO, A. Mallarmé et Victor Hugo. *RScH* n. s. fasc. 120: 515-527, oct.-déc. 1965.

More important for Mallarmé than for V. H., but illustrates the undoubted influence of V. H. on a poet who seems at first glance essentially different.

508. TROUSSON, R. Quelques aspects du mythe de Prométhée dans l'œuvre poétique de Victor Hugo. *Bulletin de l'Association Guillaume Budé* 4ᵉ. série: 86-98, mars 1963.

Gives numerous examples, showing that for V. H. Prometheus symbolized sacrifice, martyrdom, and undaunted courage. Cf. Py, no. 332.

509. COMEAU, P. T. «Le Satyre» dans la *Légende des siècles* de Victor Hugo. *FR* 39: 849-861, May 1966.

A very careful and useful critical analysis of the poem, leading, however, to no startlingly new conclusions. Cf. no. 350.

510. RIFFATERRE, M. Hugo's *Orientales* revisited. *American Society Legion of Honor Magazine*, 36 (2): 103-118, 1965.

R. argues that most critics are mistaken in viewing this volume as «a masterpiece of colorful *pittoresque*, a poetry of light». He believes rather that «the *Orientales* receive their light from the poet's inner vision», and that their colors and their exoticism are «born of his efforts to free literary language».

511. VICTOR HUGO: *L'Ane*. Édition critique par Pierre Albouy. (Cahiers Victor Hugo, no. 3) Flammarion, 1966. 345 p.

First published in 1880, *L'Ane* was conceived and written much earlier. Albouy fixes its conception and composition, places it in V. H.'s intellectual evolution and in his poetic program. «*L'Ane* assure une transition entre *Dieu* et *La Légende des siècles*, étant une méditation sur l'histoire humaine, dans la mesure où cette histoire dépend, au premier chef, du progrès moral et religieux.» Excellent critical apparatus includes, in addition to introduction, variant readings, and notes, an index of V. H.'s vocabulary.

INDEX I

AUTHORS OF FOREGOING STUDIES
NUMBERS REFER, NOT TO PAGES, BUT TO ENTRIES

Abraham, P. 357.
Alain (Chartier, E.). 204.
Albalat, A. 49.
Albouy, P. 35, 138-139, 269-270, 319, 357-358, 511.
Allem, M. 32, 50, 63.
Ambrière, F. 140.
André, L. 359.
Angrand, P. 51, 360-361, 363.
Ascoli, G. 230, 271, 427.
Asseline, A. 52.
Aubrée, E. 60, 362.
Audiat, P. 53.
Auffray, A. 141.
Avéroff, G. 467.

Bach, M. 363-365.
Baldensperger, F. 142, 207, 258, 428, 495.
Banasevic, N. 366.
Barberry, B. 367.
Barineau, E. 36, 272-273.
Barrère, J.-B. 1, 17, 54, 55, 56, 139, 143-146, 167, 176, 188, 194, 247, 251-253, 274-278, 314, 368-369, 468, 476, 486, 505, 506.
Bart, B. F. 487.
Barthou, L. 57-61, 488-489.
Baschet, R. 189.
Baudelaire, Ch. 147.
Baudoin, Ch. 148, 279.
Bauer, H. F. 280.
Bédé, J.-A. 112, 215, 309.
Bellessort, A. 149.
Béguin, A. 281, 469.
Benda, J. 490, 501.

Benoit-Guyod, G. V. 231.
Benoit-Lévy, E. 62-63, 370.
Berret, P. 19, 28, 64, 150-154, 257, 282, 283, 336, 338, 371-372, 429.
Bersaucourt, A. de 155.
Bertaut, J. 430.
Biré, E. 65-67.
Bisson, L. 25, 284, 296.
Blanchard, M. 431.
Bloch, J.-R. 204.
Born, E. 156.
Bouchet, A. du 285.
Boudout, J. 48.
Bounoure, G. 286.
Boussel, P. 68.
Braspart, M. 13.
Braun, S. D. 491.
Bray, R. 157.
Brée, G. 300.
Brombert, V. 158.
Bruneau, Ch. 254.
Brunet, G. 69, 287.
Brunot, F. 255.
Butor, M. 159, 373, 432.

Cahen, A. 151.
Camby, J. 70.
Carlson, M. 374.
Carré, J. M. 71, 214.
Cassou, J. 204.
Cellier, L. 258, 375.
Chaboseau, A. 160, 289.
Charles, P. A. 161.
Charlier, G. 72, 376, 433.
Chenay, P. 73.
Chesnier du Chesne, A. 492.

Citoleux, M. 434.
Clancier, G. E. 290.
Claudel, P. 291.
Clément-Janin, N. 74.
Collignon, A. 292.
Comeau, P. T. 509.
Constans, Ch. 293.
Cornaille, R. 162, 167.
Cousin, J. 294, 377.
Curzon, H. de 435.

Daubray, C. 11, 75, 76, 493.
David, S. 226.
Debidour, A. 436.
Debien, G. 378.
De Boer, J. P. Chr. 494.
Dédéyan, Ch. 470, 471.
Deffoux, L. 63, 77.
Delafarge, P. 295.
Delalande, J. 54, 78, 79, 163, 167.
Ditchy, J. K. 164.
Draper, F. W. M. 437, 472.
Dresse de Lebioles, P. 495.
Drouet, Juliette. 379.
Dubois, M. 68.
Dubois, P. 2, 165.
Du Bos, M. 438.
Duclaux, Mme 80.
Dumesnil, R. 380.
Dupuy, E. 81.
Duval, G. 256.

Ecalle, M. 82.
Emery, L. 166.
Escholier, R. 57, 83-86, 167, 186, 215.
Estève, E. 213.
Evans, D. O. 168, 232, 439.
Ewert, A. 254.

Flottes, P. 87.
Flutre, F. 296.
Fongaro, A. 507.
Foucher, P. 88.
Fourcassié, J. 297.
Fréminet, E. 298.
Froment-Guieyesse, G. 89.

Gaudon, J. 16, 30, 90, 153, 169, 381, 440.
Gaulmier, J. 382.
Gautier, Th. 91, 92.
Gely, C. 383.

George, A. 496.
Georgel, P. 162, 384.
Gieser, W. F. 170.
Gifford, G. H. 299.
Girard, R. 385.
Giraud, J. 386, 436, 441, 497.
Glachant, P. & V. 442.
Glauser, A. 300.
Grammont, M. 301.
Grant, E. M. 26, 171, 218, 233, 234, 240, 250.
Green, F. C. 473.
Gregh, F. 172.
Grégoire, E. 257.
Griffiths, D. A. 93.
Grillet, Cl. 94, 153, 173, 352, 498.
Guéhenno, J. 204.
Guiard, A. 174, 302.
Guillaumie-Reicher, G. 95.
Guille, F. V. 96.
Guillemin, H. 18, 23, 26, 37, 38, 41, 97-102, 109, 175-179, 303-304.
Guilloton, V. 443.
Guimbaud, L. 103-107, 305.
Gusdorf, G. 387.
Guyard, M.-F. 31, 388.
Guyau, J.-M. 180, 235.
Guyon, B. 306.

Hamelin, J. 236, 499.
Hazard, P. 108, 474.
Herford, C. H. 476.
Herscher, G. 162.
Heugel, J. 181.
Hoffmann, L.-F. 307.
Hofmannsthal, H. von 182.
Hoog, A. 197, 308.
Hooker, K. W. 183, 473.
Huard, G. 389-390, 397.
Hugo, A. 109.
Hugo, Mme V. 110.
Hugo, V. See Section III and nos. 111, 120.
Huguet, Ed. 258, 391.
Hunt, H. J. 20, 31, 168, 171, 181, 188, 237, 238, 240, 250, 253, 279, 300, 309, 336, 392, 423, 457, 461.

Isay, R. 239, 444.

Jacoubet, H. 310.
Jamet, Cl. 311.

A SELECT AND CRITICAL BIBLIOGRAPHY 91

Jasinski, R. 312.
Josephson, M. 112.
Journet, R. 14, 15, 22, 24, 27, 40, 43, 44, 139, 304, 313-316, 393-395, 446.
Joussain, A. 259.

Koyré, A. 317.
Krappe, A. H. 318.

Lacretelle, P. de 113, 234, 240, 250.
La Force, Duc de 445.
Lalou, R. 204.
Lambert, F. 446.
Lancaster, H. C. 447.
Lanson, G. 448, 455.
Larroutis, M. 319, 396.
Lebègue, R. 320.
Le Breton, A. 114, 390, 397, 449.
Le Cœur, Ch. 46.
Leconte de Lisle, Ch. 184-185.
Le Dantec, Y. G. 320.
Le Dû, A. 260-261.
Legay, T. 186.
Lesclide, J. 116.
Lesclide, R. 115.
Leuilliot, B. 398.
Levaillant, M. 47, 153, 181, 187-188, 322, 323, 450-451.
Ley-Deutsch, M. 500.
Lote, G. 452.
Lumbroso, V. 82.
Lyonnet, H. 453.

Maclean, C. M. 399-400.
Maigron, L. 401.
Mallion, J. 189.
Mann, H. 204.
Maréchal, C. 190.
Marmier, J. 191-192.
Marsan, J. 21, 34, 117, 193.
Martin, E. L. 262.
Martinenche, E. 456, 474.
Maurin, M. 300, 324.
Maurois, A. 118.
Maury, P. 287, 325.
Mélèze, J. 42.
Messac, R. 402.
Messières, R. de 109, 119.
Meurice, P. 11, 120.
Meyer, E. 263.
Michaux, F. 3, 280.

Milhaud, G. 357, 403.
Montargis, J. 454.
Moore, O. H. 194, 404-407, 423, 455.
Moraud, M. 475.
Moreau, P. 48, 195, 241, 326-327.
Morel-Fatio, A. 456, 481.
Mornet, D. 157, 171.
Mouquet, J. 328.

Page, F. 405, 408.
Partridge, E. 476.
Péès, S. 409.
Péguy, Ch. 196, 329.
Pendell, W. D. 457.
Peoples, M. 121.
Peter, R. 122.
Peyre, H. 330.
Philipot, E. 410.
Picard, R. 242.
Picon, G. 35.
Pietri, F. 477-481.
Piroué, G. 411.
Pommier, J. 243, 306, 379, 390, 397, 412-414.
Pouilliart, R. 40.
Poulet, G. 197-198.
Prinet, J. 5.
Pruner, F. 331.
Purnal, R. 42, 458.
Py, A. 139, 332.

Raymond, M. 199, 204, 286, 333.
Refort, L. 264.
Remigereau, F. 415, 497.
Renouvier, Ch. 181, 200, 334.
Ricatte, R. 357, 416-417.
Riffaterre, M. 15, 24, 176, 194, 201-203, 315, 335, 459, 461, 510.
Rigal, E. 336-338, 460.
Rinsler, N. 339, 482.
Robert, G. 14, 15, 18, 22, 24, 27, 40, 41, 43, 44, 304, 313-316, 340, 393-395.
Robertson, M. E. I. 238, 264, 475.
Rochette, A. 265.
Rolland, R. 204.
Roos, J. 205, 418.
Rousselot, J. 206.
Rozelaar, L. 244-245.
Rudwin, M. 4, 207.
Rushworth, F. D. 246.
Russell, O. W. 461.

Saint-Denis, E. de 208.
Saulnier, V. L. 209.
Saurat, D. 204, 210-212, 419.
Savey-Casard, P. 20, 247-249, 250, 359.
Schenck, E. M. 213.
Schinz, A. 250.
Schneider, P. 341.
Schwab, R. 214, 483.
Séché, L. 123-124.
Sée, H. 462.
Seebacher, J. 44, 342, 357, 394-395, 420-422, 423, 461.
Seillière, E. 475.
Sergent, J. 6, 7, 125, 167, 215, 501.
Seznec, J. 214.
Shortliffe, G. 502.
Simaika, R. 423.
Simon, G. 11, 33, 126-130, 424, 463.
Solente, S. 5.
Souchon, P. 131-135, 343.
Soupault, Ph. 204.
Souriau, M. 39, 425, 464.
Spencer, Ph. 20.
Stapfer, P. 136, 216, 344.
Steele, A. J. 36.
Surer, P. 56.

Temple-Patterson, H. 217-218, 266, 345-346, 405, 440.

Tersen, E. 357, 426.
Thibaudet, A. 219-220.
Thiébaut, M. 221.
Thierry, J.-J. 42.
Thomas, J. H. 484.
Thouvenin, G. 347-348, 485.
Tiersot, J. 503.
Tint, J. 222.
Tortel, J. 223.
Tournier, G. 434, 465.
Trousson, R. 508.
Truchet, J. 29.

Uitti, K. D. 349.
Ullmann, E. de 267.
Ullmann, S. 268.

Venzac, G. 20, 45, 59, 62, 137, 165, 224, 225, 227, 247.
Vial, A. 319, 350.
Vianey, J. 22, 351-352, 466.
Viatte, A. 226, 227, 317, 353-354.
Vinchon, J. 228.
Vivier, M. 504.
Voisine, J. 309.

Weber, J.-P. 229.
Wilson, N. 355.

Zumthor, P. 207, 356.

INDEX II

WRITERS AND PERSONS, OTHER THAN VICTOR HUGO,
ALSO TREATED IN THE FOREGOING STUDIES

Addison, J. 425.
Aubigné, Agrippa d'. 344.

Ballanche, P. 205, 319.
Balzac, H. de. 84, 366.
Baudelaire, Ch. 267, 325, 328, 383.
Beeverell, J. 399.
Béranger, P. 76.
Biard, Léonie. 57, 85, 105, 271, 343, 390.
Binet, E. 410, 415.
Blanc, L. 405.
Boulanger, L. 124.
Byron, Lord. 272, 338, 437.

Campbell, T. 280
Chamberlayne, E. 400.
Charlet, N. 124.
Collin de Plancy, J. 76.
Commynes, Ph. de. 391.

David d'Angers, P. 124.
Davity, P. 497.
Delacroix, E. 124, 125.
Deveria, A. & E. 124.
Drouet, Juliette. 30, 57, 60, 73, 85, 98, 103, 104, 118, 132, 135, 187, 379, 390, 414.
Du Breul, J. 391.
Du Fouilloux, J. 415.
Dumas, A. (père). 76, 84.

Fabre d'Olivet, A. 226.
Flaubert, G. 49.
Foucher, P. 88.
Fourier, Ch. 226

Gaillardet, F. 460.
Gautier, Th. 76, 84.
Gœthe, J. W. von. 142, 280, 339, 471, 495.
Grillparzer, F. 441.
Grimm, F. M. von. 466.

Herodotus. 298.
Horace, Q. 191-192.
Hugo, Adèle (i. e. V. H.'s daughter). 99, 109, 119.
Hugo, Adèle (Mme Victor Hugo). 50, 63, 77, 85, 97, 110, 129.
Hugo, François-Victor. 96, 111.
Hugo, Gen. Leopold. 58, 99.
Hugo, Sophie. 106.

Janin, J. 74.
Johannot, Ch. & T. 124.
Juvenal, D. 292.

Kauffmann, Angelica. 448.
Kohlrausch, R. 441.
Kotzebue, A. von 471.

Lacroix, P. 438.
Lamartine, A. de. 76, 405.
Lamennais, F. de. 190.
Lanvin, Blanche. 57.
Laprade, V. 319.
Leroux, P. 168, 319.
Lessing, G. 471.

Maistre, J. de. 396.
Mallarmé, S. 507.

Marx, K. 246.
Mathieu, P. 391.
Mercier, L. S. 217, 218, 266, 345, 346, 405, 408.
Meurice, P. 108, 120.
Michelet, J. 71.
Millevoye, Ch. 280.
Moore, T. 280.

Nanteuil, C. 60, 124.
Nerval, G. de. 325, 339.
Nodier, Ch. 127, 161, 213, 227, 280, 355, 504.

Planche, G. 76.
Ponson du Terrail, P. 402.
Pradier, Claire. 133.

Racine, J. 216.
Rey-Dusseuil, A. 380.
Richter, Jean-Paul. 217, 281.
Robelin, Ch. 124.

Rocoles, J. B. de. 386, 415.

Sainte-Beuve, Ch. 50, 63, 77, 84, 123, 124.
Saint-Valry, A. (Pseud. of A. Souillard). 72.
Sand, G. 288.
Sauval, H. 391.
Schiller, J. 280, 471.
Schœlcher, V. 93.
Schreiber, A. 441.
Scott, W. 280, 401, 437.
Shakespeare, W. 40, 335, 437, 489.
Staël, Mme de. 471.
Sue, E. 402.

Troyes, J. de. 391.

Vacquerie, A. 108, 117.
Vergil, P. 174.
Vigny, A. de. 61, 76, 81, 126, 434.
Weill, A. 152.

The Department of Romance Studies Digital Arts and Collaboration Lab at the University of North Carolina at Chapel Hill is proud to support the digitization of the North Carolina Studies in the Romance Languages and Literatures series.